AFRICA
Its Music & Its People

Pascal Bokar
Thiam, Ed.D.

Magueye Seck, Ph.D.

Foreword by Archbishop
Franzo W. King, D.D.
Saint John Coltrane
African Orthodox Church.

D0118412

Charleston, SC
www.PalmettoPublishing.com

Africa; Its Music & Its People
Copyright © 2022 by Pascal Bokar Thiam, Ed.D.

All rights reserved
No portion of this book may be reproduced, stored in a retrieval system, or transmitted in any form
by any means–electronic, mechanical, photocopy, recording, or other–except for brief quotations in
printed reviews, without prior permission of the author.

First Edition

Hardcover: 979-8-88590-052-2
Paperback: 979-8-88590-053-9
eBook: 979-8-88590-435-3

DEDICATION

This book is dedicated to my parents Abdou and Noelle Thiam who always stressed the importance of education, culture and travel. My parents raised my sisters and me in an environment of complete racial harmony seven years before Hollywood's Guess Who is Coming for Dinner was considered experimental. I discovered race and its impact outside of my parents' home. Growing up in West Africa and going to school there, I was taught about Africa and Africans, its history or lack thereof by the French colonial academic system…and the branding began…

Coming to America to pursue a career as a Jazz guitarist for the sole purpose of finding my dream gig playing in a big band behind Sammy Davis, Jr, Dean Martin or Frank Sinatra in Las Vegas and marrying a pretty cocktail waitress, I had zero intention of embracing an academic career to reflect upon my continent or my cultural upbringing until crossing Mass Avenue in Boston at 2 am in the morning when from a car rushing to hit me in that cold and clear night, the N…. word was hurled… a word I knew nothing about… and in its ringing echo, the burgeoning discovery and journey into a world's perception of me… as a man of African descent…

Foreword

We are quite fortunate and well served as students and scholars who find ourselves in search of trusted knowledge, information and clarity concerning matters of most importance regarding the continent of Africa and its contributions in the reading of this book so aptly titled *Africa; Its Music and Its People*. What better source of information could one hope for, then to be favored with scholars from the African continent. Dr. Pascal Bokar Thiam a respected authority on the subject matters here discussed and Dr. Magueye Seck together begin filling a cultural, academic and political void that has too long been overlooked and undervalued.

We only have gratitude for this well written book and can only encourage the study of such works as we look forward to the future editions of such a book as well as the addition of equally trusted scholars of African descent to continue expressing their valuable cultural and academic knowledge and perceptions of all matters of insights concerning the continent of Africa. Many thanks and appreciation to the authors.

The Most Reverend Franzo W. King, D.D.
Archbishop & Patriarch,
Saint John Coltrane African Orthodox Church

Reviews

Very few artists-educators can tread the waters of knowledge between Jazz, social justice, and cognitive psychology. Dr. Pascal Bokar Thiam does so with ease. A respected performer, educator, Dr. Thiam has played with the best of them: Dizzy Gillespie, Donald Byrd and others...his knowledge of Africa's music and culture is just as extensive as his knowledge for the music of America. And he shows us that it is one music. One Love,

Teodross Avery, DMA.
Faculty, Music Department
California State University Dominguez Hills, CA

In my review of this well written and beautiful book, I considered it to be the blueprint for African art and music. As a fine artist and clinical psychologist, this book is truly a revelation to the true meaning of art, music and life. I have also used music as a therapeutic tool to help my patients to heal their hurts and relive life. Reading this book: *Africa; Its Music and Its People* is to me the process of upstanding our internal musical instilled in all of us from conception to the end of life: The "heart beat" music is life and life is music which is rooted from the mother continent Africa. I strongly recommend to everyone the book *Africa; Its Music and Its People*...

Alioune Cissokho, PhD. MFA.
Clinical Psychologist/Art therapist
Rhode Island School of Design, Providence. RI
Northeastern University, Boston, MA

Accomplished Malian and Senegalese musician and intellectual Dr. Pascal Bokar Thiam decolonizes the vast musical histories of the African continent with indigenous and Africa-centered perspectives of their enduring cultural, political, and economic relevance. Dr. Thiam provides a cultural re-mapping of the continent into five distinct geographic and cultural regions, and then links musical styles and instrumentation —from talking drums to the kalimba— to specific ethnic, language, and religious groups. Covering a broad range of musical innovators and luminaries from Ali Farka Toure to Fela Kuti, his work deconstructs legacies of misinformation and eurocentrism and connects African musical cultural production to the decolonial theorizing of Cheikh Anta Diop and Theophile Obenga, offering insight into the rhythmic intuition and pulse of Negritude. In the tradition of scholar/musicians like free jazz pioneer and author George E. Lewis, Dr. Thiam's work not only offers a decolonizing insider perspective, but it swings with the power of a work written from the heart and soul.

Nicholas L. Baham III, Ph.D.
Professor and Chair
Department of Ethnic Studies
California State University East Bay

Table of Contents

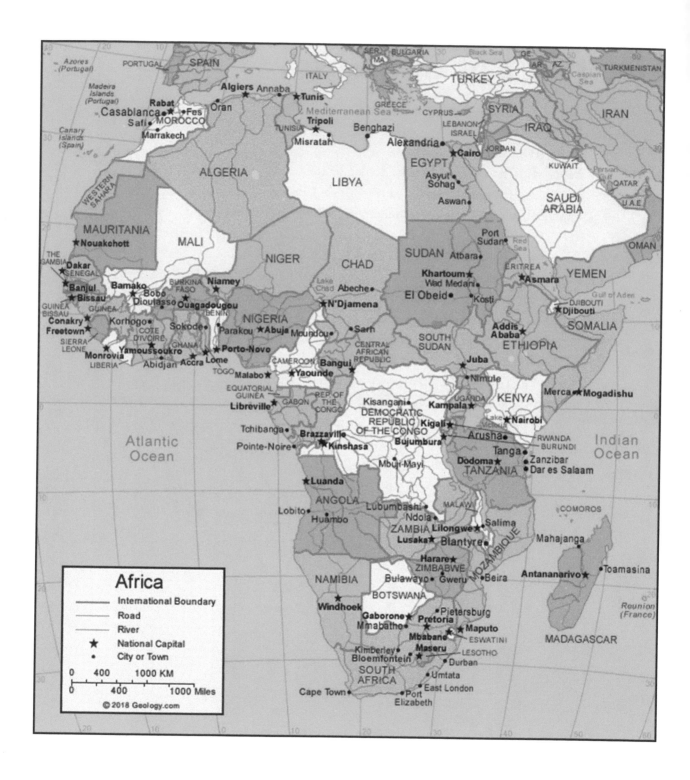

Introduction

Africa, the continent where humanity began, its wonders, its majesty, its variety, its cultural diversity, the warmth and the genius of its humanity cannot be summarized in a book or even in dozens of books but there is a need today to begin the Herculean process of compiling and organizing from an African perspective the synthesis of our human knowledge and heritage. This book is the beginning of that process. It is an attempt to organize our African musical heritage by nations and cultures with some historical information about the socio cultural and political perspectives that may have shaped the historical contexts and therefore influenced the directions of the music of the continent over time.

Music is an expression of cultural power and African music reflects that might in all of its glory and its diversity, astonishing in its variety, always rooted in tradition, constantly open to horizons and always, but always anchored in the rhythmic intuitive nature of Africans' subconscious expression of a ternary subdivision of time from which the musical term "swing" comes from. The cultural power of Africa resides in the rhythmic intuitive expression of the culture of its humanity on the continent, and in the diaspora and over the centuries it has become clear that while in some historical instances Africans left Africa, Africa never left them and wherever Africans went... African culture went...

Most of what had been written about Africa, its cultures and its music had been written in the 18th, 19th and 20th century by individuals not issued from African communities, individuals who could not speak the African languages and were not proficient in African music let alone African instrumental music and rhythms and although some were well intended the majority of their written work except for very few exceptions reflected in their choice of vocabulary and academic conclusions the prejudices and biases of the pre-colonial, colonial and neo-colonial periods inflicted upon the continent.

While the Atlantic Slave Trade has been documented as one of humanity's most injurious holocausts in its scope, duration and purpose, one must remind younger generations about the enormously damaging impact and destabilizing factor the Berlin Conference of 1884 convened by Germany's Chancellor Otto Von Bismarck inflicted upon Africa's socio cultural, historical, political and economic balance. The Berlin conference of the European colonial powers drew for the purpose of their own economic interests the incredibly Machiavellian territorial borders the continent of Africa inherited and the socio cultural, economic, military and political consequences and ills its current populations have to manage and unravel on a daily basis.

What the music of Africa shows is that it cares not about administrative borders, it has its own organic, natural, socio cultural and ancestral boundaries borne out of the geography of the continent, the lives and livelihood of its people defined by the winds of climate change and the migrations of its population groups and if you listen carefully African music will speak to you about the resilience and the genius of its people, their aspirations and their sorrows, their determination and their hopes. African music will whisper to you about the socio cultural and political events that have happened or are happening on the continent that even the press does not know about or sometimes cannot report.

Africa is the custodian of this mystery we call humanity and its music is the sonic message of its divinity...

Chapter 1

Africa; An Overview

Africa, the second-largest continent with approximately11.7 million square miles including adjacent islands, covers 6% of Earth's total surface area or 20% of its land area. As of 2018, it was the second most populous continent with 1.3 billion People. This represents 16% of the world's population and also the youngest. This very young population has a median age of 19 years old compared to a worldwide median age of 30.

Africa is the richest continent on Earth. Its unimaginable mineral resources in uranium, cobalt, oil, gold, silver, chromium, copper, manganese, palladium, titanium, diamonds, platinum etc… have made it the envy of the rest of the world and Europe in particular. As a result, the continent has had to suffer multiple socio cultural catastrophes (Davidson, 1980)[1] including but not limited to the Atlantic Slave Trade, multiple European colonial invasions (Berlin Conference of 1884), and the legacies of the Cold War.

Today, the continent continues to battle the economic and financial consequences of a neo-colonialism paradigm couched under a new terminology called globalization that has become synonymous with the terminologies and ideologies governing the concepts of domination, exploitation, and oppression when talking to African populations on the ground. These constant external frictions from neo-colonial powers trying to access Africa's mineral resources by any means necessary are the primary causes of the continent's inability to elect its own stable and far-sighted governance.

Africa is boarded to the north by the Mediterranean Sea with an opening to the Atlantic Ocean via the strait of Gibraltar, the Isthmus of Suez (construction beginning as early as 1854 the Red Sea to the northeast, the Indian Ocean to the southeast and the Atlantic Ocean to the west. The continent includes the massive island of Madagascar and various archipelago (Seychelles, Zanzibar etc.). As of today, the continent of Africa counts 54 independent states and a number of territories. The West African country of Nigeria (former colony of Great Britain is the largest by population (201 million) and Algeria is Africa's largest country by surface area (919,595 square miles).

The African Union, was a glimmer of hope and unity promulgated by Africa's first pan Africanist scholar and prime minister of the country of Ghana (formerly Gold Coast) Dr. Nkwame Krumah. He led the establishment of the African Union headquartered in Addis Ababa, Ethiopia.

---

1   Davidson, Basil. *Africa Series*. Davidson Collection, 1984.

The African Union was created to allow African member countries to plan and coordinate economic, politic and military approaches to address issues and challenges of continental consequences, in their proportions and scope.

Africa straddles the Equator. While the majority of the continent and its countries are in the Northern Hemisphere, it has a significant number of countries in the Southern Hemisphere. Its biodiversity is baffling in scope and it is the continent with the largest number of animal, insect, and plant species in the world. Given its size the continent is also widely affected by environmental issues such as droughts, and global warming which contribute actively to the widening desertification of the Sahara to the north of the continent and expansion of the Kalahari desert to the South, including but not limited to man-made deforestation, water scarcity, sprawling urbanization, local and western nations imported waste etc. Climate change has had a great impact on the continent and its scientists are working overtime to try to mitigate the challenges and ecological consequences of such climatic consequences.

Africa is the birthplace of humanity. The scope of humanity's birthplace extends from the Ethiopian plateau of Hadar to the region of the Great Lakes, to Tanzania and South Africa. This information has been verified by the scientific community since the beginning of the 20th century after the discoveries of British/Kenyan Drs. Louis and Mary Leakey (Leakey, 1934)[23] and confirmed by Drs. Johanson and Gray (Johanson, Gray, 1981)[4] and again in the 21st century through the works of Dr. Jeremy Thomson (Thomson, 2000).[5]

From early humanoids named Lucy approximately 3.2 million years in Hadar, Ethiopia to the possibly even older South African fossils discovered by Drs. Way and Herries (Herries, Way 2020)[6], Africa and its eastern and southern parts have been recognized as the locations of origins of our human cradle. Historically, it was established that the earliest high civilizations in Antiquity had grown from Africa and had begun with the Nubians (Sudanese of today) in the Eastern part of the continent, and the Egyptians in the northeastern part but we are now finding evidence of high civilization in West Africa (Mali) predating the Nubians and Egyptians (Gus Casely Hayford, 2010).[7]

Dating 10,000 years BC, vestiges of advanced pottery indicative of highly evolved human civilizations were found in the Bandiagara Region of today's Mali. The pyramids of Giza, Egypt are 3250 years BC. In 2017, the government of Sudan (ancient Nubia) stated that its pyramids were 2000 years older than those of Egypt. The time lag and the archeological and cultural evidence of high civilizations presence from West Africa, Mali 10,000 years BC all the way to the East to Sudan and Egypt is overwhelming and who could overlook the Sphinx, this enormous majestic feline like carving whose carbon dating nuclear datation

2   Leakey, L.S.B. *Some Aspects of the Kikuyu Tribe*. Man, 34,59, 1934.

3   Leakey, L. S. B., Leakey, M. *Recent discoveries of fossil hominids in Tanganyika: At Olduvai and near Lake Natron*. Current Anthropology, 6, 422-424, 1965.

4   Johanson, Donald, and Maitland Edey. *Lucy: The Beginnings of Humankind*. New York: Simon and Schuster, 1981.

5   Thomson, Jeremy. *Humans Did Come Out of Africa,*. Journal Nature, 2000.

6   Way, Amy & Herries, Andy. *Australopithecus, Paranthropus*. Australian Museum, 2020.

7   Casely-Hayford. *Gus. Lost Kingdoms of Africa*. BBC Series 4, 2010.

places it at around 9000 BC. Imagine the size and grandeur of the civilizations that built the Sphynx!

One of the great historical academic falsifications still alive today has been the baffling effort by Western academics to disconnect socio culturally thus racially Egypt from Nubia (Sudan), and from its continent Africa, hence the fabrication of the geo-political term "Middle East". Everybody knows that there isn't a middle of anything on a sphere. This futile academic/political agenda to claim Egypt as a non-African civilization is clearly a testimony to the significance of Egypt's cultural, scientific, mathematical and spiritual magnificence. While in the construct of chronology of civilizational cultural foundations race may matter, respect for chronology must matter.

There is a simple thing western academia does not seem to understand when it comes to Africa, namely the place of Black people in the story of humanity's development and that's the concept of chronology. Let me try to explain it this way, Africans were the first on the planet, Africans were Black, therefore Black Africans gave birth to humanity in its entirety (Africans built the foundational concepts of civilization from science to spirituality for the rest of humanity to borrow, why? Again, because Black Africans were the first on the planet...hence chronology...

However, these same western academics stop right at Egypt for they cannot explain Nubia, south of Egypt. Nubia (current Sudan) was the well known and established socio cultural and scientific aquifer that fed Egypt. Nubians are so dark in skin tones that it completely defeats any European purpose of trying to portray the ancient Egyptians as Europeans/Caucasians hence the failed Hollywood mythology of lovely Liz Taylor becoming a Pharaoh of Egyptians etc... While it is important to recognize that there has been a significant migration of populations from

Arab nations into Northern Egypt since the 7th century it is in the scale of humanity's chronology and certainly Black Africa a recent migration phenomenon. Migrating Arab populations were not the cultural foundation of the Egypt of Antiquity, they were not their Pharoahs and never were the engineers or architects of such a civilization. The Greek scholar Herodotus who was himself an eyewitness described the Egyptians without ambiguity "as very Black with woolly hair" (Finch, 1987)[8] and you would have to be on some serious controlled substances to believe that this was the description of a Caucasian.

University professors Drs. Cheikh Anta Diop of Senegal and Theophile Obenga of Congo demonstrated time and time again as early as the 1960s, both scientifically and through the etymology of the linguistic process that Egypt was an entire part of cultural Black Africa (Diop 1953)[9] and that Egypt owed its civilizational heights to African populations from sub Saharan origins (Davidson 1980). The 1974 Cairo Conference on Egyptology saw a masterclass given by the African professors Diop and Obenga to a large audience of Egyptologists on the Black African origins of Egyptian culture of Antiquity. Scientists present at the conference were left baffled and the pseudo academic attempt to Europeanizing the Egypt of Antiquity has been in a state of seizure ever since.

The massive immigration into northern Africa by populations from Arabic countries such as Irak, Syria and the Arabic Peninsula on the northern part of the African continent is in term of chronology of migration a recent mass phenomenon. The evidence of that is in the etymology of the term

8   Finch, Charles III. *The Black Roots of Egypt's Glory*. Washington Post, Oct 11,1987.

9   Diop, Cheikh Anta. *The Cultural Unity of Negro Africa*. Paris: Subsequent English Edition, 1959.

that the Greeks gave to people of Black skin living in the northern part of Africa i.e. "Moors" which means Black in Greek and not "White with a tan" or Arab as some of my Westerner friends pretend, for the Greeks themselves are "Whites with a tan" and they never called themselves "Moors"... for they knew better...

What is true however, is that the splendors of Egyptian and Nubian cultures create a conundrum for the European colonial ideology of White supremacy and there is a reason why there are no pyramids in Greece or in Macedonia. That reason is that Africans in general but specifically Egyptians and Nubians did not trust the Greeks or the Romans who came and studied for hundreds of years in Africa and that is why they never shared with them the mathematical formulas that allowed for the construction of these architectural African feasts of technology that we call pyramids.

Unlike some flawed history channels on television would like you to believe, no green Martians built the pyramids, Africans did, and these African scholars and high priests kept the mathematical formulas away from the Greeks and the Romans through the African process and wisdom of the oral tradition through the initiation of the selected worthy, otherwise you would have pyramids in Greece and elsewhere in Europe twice the size of those of Giza. Why? You might ask, because it is in human nature...to compete...

Chapter 2

Africa; The Historical & Political Context

Africa, where human civilization began and yet as one of its noted scholars Dr. Augustus Casely Hayford remarked "we know less about this continent than anywhere else in the world" and this is where we need to begin when we talk about Africa. The statement from Dr. Casely Hayford needs to be taken very seriously for it gives us all a context for the examination of that reality. Why don't we know more about Africa since it is where humanity began?

The answer is both simple and complex. Simple, because reality has observed that national politics drive the agenda of education and academic scholarship and that the Western powers who dominated the economic and technological landscape had no vested political interest in hailing Africa and African culture previous majestic heights. Yet, it is true that Africans invented linear writing. Nubians wrote before anyone else and Egyptians wrote scientific essays on papyrus, formulas of chemistry, precepts of medicine, protocols of surgery on humans and animals, poetry, and legal briefs. The term "alphabet" itself is a combination of African words (Obenga, 1973).[10]

They wrote laws and judgments, advanced concepts of mathematics both algebraic and abstract, they wrote essays in geometry, in physics, in astronomy. We use their calendar system today. These Africans wrote about affairs of the State, practices related to land management matters, they wrote about currency exchanges and commercial practices. They wrote about military strategies and religious concepts using both emic and etic perspective contexts to define their languages and cultures through the prism of the dynamics of symbolism and their hermeneutics.

As early as 2700 BC they had invented the paper but as a general rule in accordance with long existing African traditions, the oral tradition was the preferred mode of transmission of knowledge for it allowed for the process of initiation to take place. Initiation of individuals as a process of selection allowed knowledge to be disseminated to those individuals who had been subjected to the rituals of initiation and had been deemed worthy of that knowledge by the high priests of Africa. There is an intuitive belief on the continent of Africa, west, north, east, south and center that

---

10 Obenga, Theophile. *Ancient Egypt and Black Africa: A Student's Handbook for the Study of Ancient Egypt in Philosophy, Linguistics and Gender Relations.* London: Karnak House, 1992.

with knowledge comes responsibility and as such not all knowledge should be made available to all and/or transmitted freely.

In 1939, scholar Sigmund Freud wrote a disturbing book entitled "Moses & Monotheism"[11] about the monumental impact of these African populations of Egypt and Nubia and how the Greeks, European culture and the entire Judeo Christian communities borrowed from African cultural, technological and spiritual concepts as he explains why the Father of a European thought i.e. Alexander the Great built his capital Alexandria not in Greece or Macedonia but in Africa, in Egypt because it was the center of academic, scientific, technological and spiritual human know how.

Almost fifty years later, in 1974, at the UNESCO Conference of Cairo, Egypt, university professors and Drs. Cheikh Anta Diop[12] and Theophile Obenga reaffirmed Dr. Freud's (1939) disturbing statements to Western academia armed with incontrovertible experiments based on nuclear physic and rooted in science. As a result of that conference miffed Western scholars began using the term "Afrocentric" to anyone in academia who dared defining humanity's socio cultural, political, spiritual and technological progress from the logical vantage point of humanity's chronology, as if Europe had ever been considered the beginning of civilizations when it has been in actuality the full beneficiary and stands on the shoulders of all of the African socio cultural and civilizational might and scientific contributions. Did the Greek Pythagoras really deserve to have the laws of triangles attached to his name for our children to remember when the only civilizations who demonstrated the mastery of the laws of geometry attached to triangles are the Nubians first and the Egyptians

second, some 4,000 years before Pythagoras was even a concept and Freud tells us that Pythagoras spent 27 years studying in Egypt? Has anyone seen a single pyramid in Greece, in the Arabic Peninsula, in Irak, in Turkey, in Italy, in Germany, in England, in Spain, in France? Sorry I forgot…there is one in Paris in the middle of the Louvre Museum built in 1989 by a Chinese American architect by the name of I.M. Pei. It is not a pyramid. In reality, it look more like a big Native American tipi covered with glass… so you get the point…so how did the laws of triangle suddenly become attached to the Greek Pythagoras for the last 150 years in western academia? We must be honest and recognize that this is just another flagrant example of western appropriation of African science in this case, geometry and I am not even raising all the "borrowing" issues associated with Euclides, Thales etc…and their so called "discoveries" all of whom studied in Egypt for years (Freud, 1939). So today, these so called western scholars who are still trying to disconnect Egypt from Black African culture would try to make you believe that it is the populations from countries from Europe or the "Middle East", those who demonstrably never built a single pyramid in their entire existence on the planet, who were the pharaohs of Egypt. It would be laughable if it wasn't so sad, particularly when academia knows full well that Nubians (Nubia current Sudan located south of Egypt) are the only human group known to have built pyramids some older that those of Egypt and that Nubians are undeniably Black Africans. This shows that racism is alive and still thriving in western academia. These continuous kinds of western academic slights against Africans and people of African descent are what contribute to a general feeling of exhaustion on the continent and

---

11 Freud, Sigmund. *Moses & Monotheism*. Knopf Publisher, 1939.
12 Diop, Cheikh Anta. *The African Origin of Civilization: Myth or Reality*. New York: L Hill, 1974.

in the Diaspora. Another scary example of supreme and willful disinformation was that of the National Aeronautics and Space Administration or NASA and this one I witnessed in my lifetime growing up in Senegal, West Africa in 1970. For all the talks in education departments all over the United States about the needs for Science, Technology, Engineering, and Mathematics programs or STEM and all the bla bla around what to do about these boys and girls of African descent who are not doing well in schools, in mathematics, sciences, physics, computer technology etc…all the meanwhile NASA never bothered to inform us until 2018 that it was an entire division of African American women mathematicians under the leadership of another African American genius by the name of Dr. Katherine Johnson who were responsible for hand calculating the elliptical orbital mechanics that allowed for the successful landing on the moon and re-entries into the atmosphere of the various unmanned and manned missions to the moon at a time when computers were in their infancy and verifiably unreliable. For 50 years this amazing feat of mathematical and scientific prowess by these Black women were kept a secret from all and in the process the western media robbed every young boy and girl on the planet and certainly those of African descent of such a major mathematical contribution and world academic recognition (Melfi, Schroeder, 2017). In 1970, NASA sent to Senegal the three astronauts (Neil Armstrong, Buzz Aldrin, Michael Collins) who landed on the Moon as part of a tour celebrating American exceptionalism. The Education department in Dakar, Senegal gave us the day off from middle school so that my classmates

and I could go witness and wave at this triumph of human technological feat of epic proportion and the image of accomplishment that was introduced in our young malleable African minds was that of three European American men…no one bothered to tell us that the geniuses who hand calculated the mathematics to send them to the moon and bring them back safely to earth, on that bus they sat in called Apollo 11, were members of an entire division composed exclusively of women of African descent, no one…and it took NASA 50 years for that academic revelation to surface…50 years something I witnessed…in my lifetime…and where is the outrage?

A complex answer, because the dynamics of power having shifted to Europe and the West in the last 400 years, Africans who were the first on the planet and never thought about the need to define themselves found themselves being defined in the literature and in pseudo sciences by a European economic and political agenda who began aggressively mounting a campaign to dominate Africa and the rest of the world at the beginning of the 17th century building from a scholarship these European nations had gained from Africa through the knowledge made available through the numerous universities built in Andalusia by the Moors which explains why Spain and its neighboring Portugal became the first medieval superpowers of Europe.

The Atlantic Slave Trade conducted by European powers as early as the 16th century with Spain and Portugal first followed by the Dutch, French and British second, and with the complicity of many African kings and communities, has remained an ugly stain in the history of humanity with long lasting socio cultural and economic consequences still alive in Africa today but also living in the Diaspora as we speak. There are many books that treat this subject with the required scholarship, passion and the appropriate disgust for the depth of its inhumanity (Horton, 2003)[13].

Our interest in the impact of the Slave Trade here seeks to inform the readers about the scope of its cultural impact through the transfer of socio cultural and musical aesthetics that occurred as a result of the forced migrations of Africans to the Americas, North, Central and South during the Slave Trade. The introduction of West African culture and music for 400 hundred years as a result of the Slave Trade shaped the identities of the cultures and the musics of the Americas, North, Central and South including that of the Caribbean.

The introduction of the Malian Ngoni (ancestor of the banjo) by West Africans in the Americas and the Caribbean allowed these African populations to use their ancestral African instrument as a vector of cultural and musical retention to maintain specific tonalities that European musicologists termed "Blue Notes" from their peculiar sonic absence from the repertoire of Bach and Mozart. These blue notes and tonal identity markers contributed to the development of North America's most influential sonic landscape called the Blues at the turn of the 20th century from which Gospel, Jazz, Rhythm & Blues, RocknRoll and Soul music will spring from. The socio cultural reality of the Atlantic Slave Trade is that wherever Africans went…Africa went…(Thiam, 2011).[14]

The winds of democratic principles that began animating Western scholars and the poor masses of Europe coupled with the widely unpopular excesses and opulence of their respective monarchies led to the dismantling of Europe's

---

13 James Oliver Horton, Lois E. Horton. *Slavery and the Making of America*. Oxford University Press, 2005.
14 Thiam, Pascal. *From Timbuktu to the Mississippi Delta*. San Diego: Cognella, 2013.

ruling class from Russia to France, England, and the rest of Western Europe. The intellectual elite of the times Danton, Marat, Robespierre, Philippe D'Orleans, including Europe's greatest fencer, violinist, composer and military genius of African and French descent the Chevalier de Saint George along with the British abolitionist Society decidedly accelerated the pace of social change in Europe thus impacting the conditions of indentured servitude and slavery worldwide leading to their ultimate demise.

Although slavery was abolished by France's first republic in 1794, it was re-instated in 1802 by Napoleon Bonaparte, who later crowned himself emperor of that country. His dismal loss at Waterloo at the hands of the British Navy sent him into exile to the island of Santa Helena, a small rock in the middle of the Atlantic ocean off the coast of West Africa so that he could ponder for the rest of his life, the magnitude of his role, duplicity and complicity in this odious human trade and tragedy we call the Atlantic Slave Trade.

Slavery was replaced by colonialism. An intellectual and economic arm of European supremacy it consisted in annexing as many territories worldwide as possible. The advent of the firearm by Europeans made territorial conquests that much easier. The systematic decimation of indigenous populations from the Americas, to the Caribbean, Africa, Australia, New Zealand, and Asia began along with the imposition of European languages and cultures throughout the globe. Along with this plague came another one namely the Western political agenda and its financing of pseudo academic description of indigenous nations, cultures and spirituality so to enable Africans to learn about Africa and themselves through the prism of a uniquely unqualified European and Western lens.

The burgeoning economic pillage of Africa created so much infighting between European powers that it forced Germany's Chancellor Otto Von Bismarck to call a conference in Berlin in 1884 to discuss and put in place an agreement that would create the conditions for a more peaceful and effective carving out of the continent. While most European powers were present and took part in what was described by King Leopold of the Belgians the carving out of "this magnificent African cake" the invited United States did not take part in such an endeavor probably having enough trouble at home managing the dynamics of its own indigenous and multi ethnic populations.

At the turn of the 20th century, European powers in fighting intensified and required African soldiers participation i.e. "Tirailleurs Senegalais" (who actually were drafted from all parts of French African colonies) to help the French fight against Germany not once but twice. This European infighting led to the disturbing human catastrophes that resulted from the carnages of World War I and World War II and the introduction of biological weapons and the horrors of the atomic bombs unleashed on Hiroshima and Nagazaki by the United States. European colonial powers also saw the arrival on the world stage of a new multiethnic friction laden, economic, political and military power named the United States of America. It was only with the indomitable courage of the Soviet Union troops pressing from the European eastern front that the United States were able to defeat the Nazi regime of the German Third Reich led by the sociopath Adolph Hitler. At the end of World War II, returning soldiers from the colonies of Africa, Asia and the Middle East began mounting social frictions and indigenous rebellions demanding independence from their respective European colonial powers. Between 1945 and

1965 the colonies' battles for independence raged on and by 1965 colonialism as a de facto political and administrative system was abandoned by European powers but only to morph into a new form of neo-colonialism or what some call today globalization accelerating economic extraction and exploitation of the mineral resources of the African continent.

Opposing socio-economic and political ideologies of development between the victors of World War II, namely the United States and the Soviet Union, created a political climate in the colonies that forced them to take sides. Given that the socio economic ills that defined colonialism were still alive and well namely, oppression, exploitation and domination, the nascent African independence movements had to choose between Western capitalism or some form of Soviet Marxist doctrines (Communism, Leninism or Socialism). The leader of the newly independent nation of India (independence wrestled from the British Crown) and founder of the Non Violence Movement Mohandas Gandhi, who had fought in South Africa against the apartheid regime to improve laws solely directed to Indians, proposed the concept of the Non Aligned nations. The entire continent of Africa became the new battlefield for economic, political and military armed conflicts agitated by Western Europe former colonial nations and the United States of America versus the nascent African independence movements with the help of the tiny but mighty Island of Cuba and the Soviet Union republics.

A group of young revolutionaries led by Fidel Castro who was successful in overthrowing the US –backed military dictatorship of the Batista regime of the Caribbean island of Cuba began organizing a new government who preached about a new political and economic doctrine entitled "Internationalism" in which all nations were invited to help each other selflessly in a spirit of brotherhood. The icons of the Internationalism doctrine were Fidel Castro, Dr. Ernesto Che Guevara, Raul Castro and Juan Almeida. Given that Fidel Castro and his Cuban revolutionaries had been successful in overthrowing the US supported Batista regime, African movements seeking their independence away from European colonial powers sought their advice and know how. While the European powers and the United States derided the efforts of the nascent African independence movements, the young Cuban leaders responded favorably to the African nations' pleas for help as early as the 1960s and a worldwide political, economic and military struggle began (El Tahri, 2006).

The government of Cuba opened its universities to train Africans in medicine, engineering, humanities, social, physical, and military sciences for decades. Between 1965 and 1988, the Cuban government engaged over half a million Cuban soldiers and Special Forces on the African theater of operations. Cubans fought corrupt European forces in Congo, US backed mercenaries along with South Africa's apartheid military platoons tirelessly alongside African guerilla movements to help them remove the shackles of colonialism from Algeria to the north to South Africa, to Guinea Bissau to the west to Zimbabwe, Mozambique, Angola, and to the center of Africa in Congo etc…

A complete worldwide press embargo was put in place. In Senegal for example, a country celebrated for its freedom of expression, its press corps never reported that half a million Cuban soldiers and Special Forces led by Cuban commander Victor Drekke were training and fighting alongside Africans for the liberation of the continent even when the combat was taking place at its own borders with Guinea Bissau. The Cuban military side by side with the military wings of the Movement of People for the Liberation of Angola (MPLA), the Zimbabwean freedom fighters against the Ian Smith racist regime of Rhodesia, and the African National Congress (ANC) military wing forced the South African military apartheid regime and its mercenaries out of Angola, Rhodesia and Namibia and obtained the liberation of the first African President of a non-apartheid South Africa namely civil rights leader Nelson Mandela. It is not an accident that Nelson Mandela's first trip outside of Africa was to Havana, Cuba to thank Fidel Castro and the Cuban people in person for helping the continent of Africa get rid of Western colonialism and apartheid. We should note that consistent with their political ideals the victorious Cubans withdrew from African wars without taking anything. They took no rights to African mines, no rights to minerals, no rights to oil or land. The Cubans only took their dead comrades.

The Cuban odyssey in Africa is one of the most successful, selfless and celebrated human commitments to the cause of freedom and independence known on the continent. Africa owes to Cuba, the Cuban people and its leadership of committed young idealistic revolutionaries an immense debt of gratitude for the help, manpower, technical know how and military bravery Cuban Special Forces displayed alongside African freedom fighters. Such a bravery, selflessness and conviction led to the successful unraveling of Western colonial forces in Africa.

While a worldwide press embargo was in full force of silence about Cuban involvement in Africa, the contemporary musics of Africa were speaking loudly about the Cuban socio- cultural and musical presence. The popular dance musics of Africa began to embrace Cuban musical influences from West Africa, Senegal, Mali and Guinea, to the Eastern Benga music of Kenya to the Congolese musical style called 'Soukous" etc... African music was speaking about Cuban presence to Africans when the world press was not...

Academic confusion also exists as there has been a continuous attempt in certain circles of dubious academic qualities to oppose the far thinking concepts of intuition and creativity of scholar Leopold Sedar Senghor[15] to the scientific rigor of Dr. Cheikh Anta Diop when in fact to anyone who has read Senghor in depth realizes that both he and Diop are saying the same thing and praised the motherland with the same fervor all along but from a different intellectual angle. It is not an either or but a complementarity of thoughts, for both Diop and Senghor are correct in the sense that the African concepts of intuition and creativity are as much a part of and linked to the African scientific discourse and its scientific conclusions for neither concept can exist outside of each other. This ability to conceptually envision the existentialism of humanity from such a wide intellectual angle ranging from creative intuition to scientific rigor is a testimony to the incredible depth of intellectual perspectives Africans have possessed since the beginning of times.

---

15   Senghor, Leopold. *Liberte*. Paris: Seuil Editions, 1964.

Chapter 3

West African Decolonization: Solidarity, Migration and Development

Magueye Seck, Ph.D.

Introduction

Since the early 1960s, Africans have been struggling with the processes of decolonization and all its complexities and consequences. We will discuss the connection between the decolonization method and the actual migration crisis of which millions of Africans depart for Europe, America, and Asia. This article will show how the current immigration development is a dangerous undertaking that weakens the culture and the project of emergence in Africa.

Social scientists maintain that settler societies, emerging empires, and leading economies have generally welcomed immigrants, as they fill labor shortages, boost population growth, and stimulate business and trade.[16] However, in this time of economic hardship and political crisis worldwide, African immigrants and Africans of the Diasporas are being blamed for these problems. They face discrimination, racism, and violence.[17] The new discoveries of natural resources in Africa have not helped accelerate the emergence nor reduce the need to emigrate. The Africans are still struggling to find effective leadership. Theoretically, an effective African leadership would transcend into a comprehensive decolonization which in turn would bring peace and security, solidarity, and social and economic development in Africa.

This author will use a triangulation of methods, including participant observation in African immigrant settlements in Europe, the United States, and within Africa, to better describe the impact of colonization and the process of decolonization. Various sociological and political perspectives will help our analysis of the decolonization process

---

16 Castles, S. and De Haas H., and Miller, M. (2014). *The Age of Migration: International Population Movements in the Modern World.* The Guilford Press. New York, London. Fifth Edition. 55-83.

17 Seck. Magueye. « Solidarité Pour Mettre Fin à la Violence Economique au Sénégal ». Notes from the 2007 International Colloquium on Migration. University Gaston Berger. Saint-Louis. Senegal.

combined with a migration crisis. Social scientists have remained mostly silent on the decolonization questions in Africa. Effective methods to free the African continent from the evil of colonization and its consequences in the social life of the African people have not yet been developed. [18] Many theories about assimilation and accommodation have occupied the academic discourse for more than half century but without practical application to development or emergence. The fundamental fact of social life is precisely that it is social—that human beings do not live in isolation but associate with other human beings [19]. What happened to the great hope of integration and independence of Africa that world leaders have been imagining for more than half century?

Methods

Various government reports and documents have been consulted as well as writings from historians, sociologists, journalists, and economists who have studied the impact of colonization and migration in Africa. From 1659 to the present time, Africans have contributed to the documentation about realities in Africa, but not to the same extent as the colonizers. This author used a triangulation of methods, including participant observation in African immigrant settlements within Africa, and Europe, the United States and the Caribbean. The author reviewed historical materials relating to colonialism, migration, and labor focusing on West Africa, mainly dominated by French colonialism. He used semi-structured and open-ended interviews and conducted face to face interviews with key professionals and migrant respondents in Saint-Louis and Dakar, Senegal; and respondents in Barcelona and Valencia, Spain; Paris, and Geneva.

The purpose of this article is to help understand the effect of colonization and the process of decolonization in West Africa. Secondly, to investigate the ongoing migration crises, which many African scholars theorize as being one of the consequences of a failed decolonization in West Africa. As a sociologist, with a doctoral degree in social policy, the author of this article has organized the first International Colloquium on Migration at the University Gaston Berger in Saint-Louis, Senegal. Many African nations attended, including Mali, Guinea, Ivory-Coast, Morocco, Mauritania, and others. Also, France, Italy and Spain were the main European nations that responded to this colloquium. The President of Senegal, Abdoulaye Wade, and many Senegalese authorities joined this extraordinary event. Much collaboration, dialogue, academic discourse, social, political, and economic perspectives came out of this three-day event in 2007. Various sociological perspectives will help our analysis of the decolonization process along with the present migration crisis. In our analysis, we will discuss how the process of decolonization appears to be in harmony and in contradiction with the Africa's historical, social, political and economic emergence.

Sociologists are consistently challenged to answer or explain problems pertinent to the

---

18 Seck. Magueye. « Solidarité Pour Mettre Fin à la Violence Economique au Sénégal ». Notes from the 2007 International Colloquium on Migration. University Gaston Berger. Saint-Louis. Senegal.

19 Blau, Peter,M. (1977). *Inequality and Heterogeneity: A primitive Theory of Social Structure*. The Free Press. London

interrelationship between work, poverty, and health. And because the transformation of African societies by colonization continues to fascinate social scientists, the answers to many of these questions become more urgent. 1) What is decolonization? 2) Who benefits from the decolonization of Africa and how is it related to migration? 3) What has been the historical role of the African leadership in the struggle for equality and dignity of Africans and the African Diasporas? 4) How are sociologists explaining the cultural, and racial aspect of decolonization? 5) What strategies exist to secure peace and security and emergence while decolonizing the African continent?

Sociologists and historians help explain the importance of leadership during the supposedly transitional periods from colonization to decolonization. Sociology provides two distinct definitions of leadership: Instrumental leadership, and expressive leadership. They refer to "instrumental leadership" as the group leadership that focuses on the completion of task. On the other hand, "expressive leadership" is the group leadership that focuses on the group's well-being. [20] This sociological distinction in leadership will be relevant in our historical and contemporary analysis of the processes of both colonization and decolonization in West Africa.

The 1960s

The 1960s also known as the "decade of independence" raised many socio-political and economic issues about decolonization. An historical analysis of the phenomenon of decolonization can help us understand why the African leadership could not have anticipated either the current migration crisis, or the lack of emergence or economic stagnation in West Africa, despite all the natural wealth and human potential. Many political leaders like Leopold S. Senghor of Senegal, Sekou Toure of Guinea, Kwame Nkrumah of Ghana, Ouphouet Boigny of Ivory Coast, Modibo Keita of Mali, among others, had all contributed in the decolonization process in West Africa.[21] Have they succeeded? If the answer is no, why did they fail to decolonize the continent? What role did they play as leaders of the first generation of "Independent Nations?" If they have succeeded, then, what does social, political, and economic independence mean? Some argue that the question of decolonization was not a priority for the colonizers, mainly France and England. The idea of "independent Nations" was simply another method to consolidate even more power with new social and political structures. Despite the new African leadership, a great deal of power resides still in the hands of the French and the British decades after independence. Consequently, the process of decolonization continues to raise more questions around leadership, security, emergence and migration.

Earlier African Leaders and the Colonial Era

Clearly, the first African political leaders who joined the French colonizers had specific roles, mainly focusing on the completion of the tasks given to them by the French. The French had their goals and objectives and their imperialist mission even before the Berlin Conference in 1884-1885. Fourteen Western States met in the Berlin Conference and

---

20 Macionis. John. (2016). *Sociology*. Pearson. Sixteen Edition.
21 Ndao, El hadj Ibrahima. 2003. *Sénégal, Histoire des Conquêtes Démocratiques*. Les Nouvelles Editions Africaines du Senegal.

agreed both to end slavery, and facilitate imperialism.[22] The French first occupied Saint-Louis du Senegal in 1659. It was not until May 10, 1914, that the first African, Blaise Diagne, became deputy for Senegal. In other words, it took two hundred fifty-five years of complete occupation before the first African join the French Assemblée, representing Senegal. In October 19th, 1915, the Senegalese who were born in the four communes of Senegal, (Saint-Louis, Goree, Rufisque, Dakar) became French citizens. The rest of the Senegalese population who constituted a clear majority, and the people of Mali, Guinee, Ivory-cost, Togo, Mauritania, and all the other colonies were disenfranchised. Then in 1934, a second Senegalese depute Galandou Diouf, was elected. In October 21st 1945, Lamine Gueye and Leopold Sedar Senghor became depute of Senegal.[23] One can argue that with these four leaders began the process of decolonization. The Pan-Africanists would disagree. They call their role to be the process of assimilation, and that assimilation is incompatible with decolonization. Therefore, the process of decolonization has not yet begun. The question remains, what is decolonization and when does it begin, and when does it end? At the risk of missing half the story, let us begin by saying that the notion held by the colonizers that African life before the colonial period was "blank, uninteresting, brutal barbarism." [24] However interesting, we will not discuss in detail, the great diversity of Africans pre-colonial time who developed forms of centralized self-rule and empires.

In the 1950s, there were leaders who strongly supported the assimilation ideology, or continuing integration into the French colonial system, such as Senghor and Boigny. They were very optimistic about the direction in which they decided to lead the "former" African colonies. Their ideas of decolonization thru assimilation were totally rejected by Touré and Nkrumah. These two wanted to start the process of unification of the continent which would have been in contradiction with what the French had in mind. The French colonial forces clearly controlled all the factors of production – the land, the labor, and the capital. They had a complete mastery of the formula of dependency. Because of their optimism and their sense of urgency in liberating the continent, Touré and Nkrumah somewhat underestimated these neo-colonial forces. The ideas of African Unity were revolutionary to many Africans, but they were totally unacceptable to the colonizers. The French were and still not willing to liberate the continent. The norms for the French were dependency and exploitation under the watch of the new African Elite.

Nawetanism, Migration and development

Because of the work of the great African Scholar, Cheikh Anta Diop, we have a general idea about the productive forces, the means of production, the accumulation and disposal of land and labor in precolonial Africa. No social scientist has compared existing African concepts on social structures so effectively with western concepts. These examples of his analysis are: the "Nawetanism", and "The talibe". [25] Thanks to his work, we can

---

22 Mazrui, Ali. *The Africans* ∶ A triple *Heritage*. Little Brown. Boston Page:160.
23 Ndao, El Hadi Ibrahima (2003) Senegal, Histoire des Conquetes Democratiques. Les Nouvelles Edition Africaines.
24 Davidson, Basil. (1995). Africa in History. A Touchstone Book .61.
25 Diop Cheikh Anta. (1987) Precolonial *Black Africa*. Lawrance Hill Books. Page 158.

compare the socio-economic structures in Africa and Europe, and connecting the variables migration and development.

Professor Diop defined *Nawetanism* (in Wolof) as a category of peasants that do not know each other, and do not constitute a class, and are not bound by any traditional group solidarity. They are mobile because they are young bachelors who go away to look for work to accumulate a dowry with which they can return to marry in their villages and settle down permanently. What is extraordinary with the *Nawetanism* concept is that *Nawetanism* is a transitional stage in the life of a young man who goes away with a permanent intention of one day returning home. He is no man's slave; no contract could permanently bind him to the land of any lord. [26]

Furthermore, Diop analyzed the main reasons why young people needed to migrate, within the context of *newatanism*. He argued that drought and progressive exhaustion of the soil prompted *young* men of a village to spend the rainy season in a region with more water, not yet exhausted by cultivation. In Diop's sociological and economic analysis of *newatanism*, one can see without doubt, the rationale behind the modern day uncontrolled, massive, and disorganized flux of migration taking place. Diop documented the effect of the desert creeping into Black Africa. There is a direct cause and effect between monoculture and the advancement of the desert. Monoculture was a forced policy of the French colonizers to the Africans. Diop described the nature of the increased movements of the peasants as direct consequences of the failed colonial policies that impacted the ecosystem which in turned accelerated the phenomenon of *newatanism* as we know it today. He demonstrated how many of the people of the people of the Djambour and Cayor region of Senegal, today half desert, withdrew toward the Baol, while the habitants of that area, specially peasants, went off in the direction of Sin-Salum, Gambia, and Casamance, all regions located farther south and more humid. Those who decided not to leave the desert ended out in the suburbs of Dakar, constituting what Diop called the growing phenomenon of proletarianization. [27]

Then, Professor Cheikh Anta Diop tackled the concept of *Talibe* which he defined as "the believer". He stated the *Taalibe* Murid, Tidjane, and other communities, constitute not only a religious group, but a class that most fascinate sociologists. In the case of Senegal, most *Taalibes* show strong solidarity not only to their marabouts, or religious leaders, but also to their families and villages.[28] The migrant who is also a *Talibe* would very likely return to his/her place of origin. They constitute the major source of external funding after corporate investment in Senegal. They constitute a significant proportion of the Senegalese diasporas, and their economic support is called "remittance" has a huge impact in Senegal's national budget. It is very important to note that unlike the reality of *Navetanist*, the modern day *Taalibes* are often highly educated in Senegal, France, United States, England, Italy, Spain; in short, they are all over the world. They are not just Navetanists, these *taalibes* are physicians, lawyers, college and university professors, students, architects, dentists, sociologists, psychologists, economists, electrical

---

26 Diop Cheikh Anta. (1987) Precolonial *Black Africa*. Lawrance Hill Books. Page 158.
27 Diop Cheikh Anta. (1987) Precolonial *Black Africa*. Lawrance Hill Books. Page 158.
28 Diop Cheikh Anta. (1987) Precolonial *Black Africa*. Lawrance Hill Books. Page 158.

engineers, police officers, musicians, heads of states, ministers, taxi drivers, garbage collectors, journalists, and peasants and so on. The modern Taalibe may not show loyalty to a particular marabout. It is also extremely important to note that there are increasingly more women, many of them talibes, who migrate and whose remittance are significant. Remittances have become a stabilizing force worldwide, thanks to the diasporas, their labor and the willingness to support their homeland reduce the impact of the failed colonial and neocolonial policies. Still many critical questions remain:

- ◆ Why does staying in Africa seem a poorer choice for a young person than risking migration?
- ◆ Specifically, what is lacking in Africa that would give a young person hope for the future if he/she stayed?
- ◆ What brings men and women migrants to a non-African destination like Spain?
- ◆ What prospects do strangers/immigrants have for integration into European societies?
- ◆ How significant is remittance or the lack of it to the life of this current generation of African?
- ◆ How do you explain the situation in relation to the weakening/strengthening of social institutions such as schools, employment, families?

I interviewed young people in separate occasions in Senegal, France, Spain, Italy, United States, Geneva, Ivory coast and Guinea. The overwhelming majority of the respondents interviewed in this article said that staying in Africa under the present condition was not acceptable. They rejected the notion not only for economic reasons, but emotionally, psychologically, and politically. They "had enough and now they have every right to migrate". They all were willing to take the risks that come along with migration. More interestingly, they feel that they have every right, like everyone who before them who migrated and succeeded in their goals and objective. They all have to fight for food, education, health, housing, and work, and saw they have no hope, no chance in Africa. "Human rights begin with breakfast" this quip from President of Senegal, Leopold Senghor, prompts many to react in alarm.[29] According to Andrew Clapham, some see the Senghor's assertion as part of an argument that certain rights, such as the right to food, need to be properly secured before one can turn to the luxury of the right to vote or to the privilege of freedom of expression. Clapham also stated that most government today agree that there should be no prioritization among different types of rights. Different types of rights are seen to be mutually reinforcing. He agreed with many sociologists and most of the interviewees that better nutrition, health and education will lead to improvements in political freedoms and the rule of law. Similarly, there seems to be an agreement that "freedom of expression and association can ensure that the best decisions are taken to protect the rights to food, health and work." [30]

What is lacking in Africa is effective leadership, basic economic vision to provide jobs opportunities for the youth, and the moral imperative

---

29   Clapham Andrew (2007) *Human Rights*. Oxford. University Press. Page 119.
30   Clapham Andrew (2007) *Human Rights*. Oxford. University Press. Page 119.

to stop poverty and corruption. Regardless of the level of education of the respondents in this project, they hugely emphasized the problems relating to leadership locally, as well as on the continent. Their level of political sophistication explaining the lack of adequate leadership was quite remarkable. They address nepotism, favoritism, and discrimination as endemic in communities all over, and they blame the leadership. They do not have any hope about seeing the ending of corruption, and see no other alternative than to migrate. In some of these interviews, the level of emotion was extremely high, because some even disclosed suicidal tendencies. In several occasions, young migrants told this author that they have been arrested in Barcelona after trying to migrate without papers and deported back to Senegal; and they were preparing to return, and they have no fear of dying in the high sea. "Bursa or Bursakh", meaning Barcelona or death. For them, the future is migration by any means necessary, even death! There is no ambiguity about how they feel about Africa. They feel bad not just for themselves, but they also feel bad for their families. Some respondents spoke emotionally about the sacrifices their parents made, usually their mothers, for spending their life savings for the boats that take them to Europe. What they see now is injustice everywhere. They are not asking for anyone's help, or even any government opportunity. Instead they are making a demand for legality, for freedom of movement so that they can sell their labor, skilled or not. They strongly believe that only the insensible and indifferent African leadership is responsible for their situation.

Interestingly, what brings men and women to non-African destination like Barcelona is nothing less than economic despair. Why are the African not trying other African nations? This author asked the question to the President of Senegal, Abdoulaye Wade: "Mister President, why would you and the other African head of states not focus on the migration issues between the African nations themselves, and see if this would reduce the number of undocumented African taking the risk to reach Europe in search for job opportunities?" President Wade enthusiastically gave an elaborate answer to the question. He framed his answer from a Pan-Africanist perspective. He recognized they were issues between the African nations when it comes to migration. He argued that Senegal would welcome any African looking for opportunity. The paradox being that the Senegalese are looking for opportunities and are dying in the Atlantic trying to reach Europe. But President Wade also insisted that an African Economic Integration would create jobs without restrictions on freedom. He understood the elements of neo-colonization, and prioritization, but in essence he said that he would bring the issue to other African heads of states as a matter of urgency. Neo-colonization policies would do the opposite. They would not give priority to economic integration, nor would they prioritize job creation outside the economic planning that the powerful nations have for Africa. Another paradox is that the powerful nations' failure to provide job opportunities for Africans in Africa create the influx of undocumented Africans on the shores of Europe and America.

The prospects these African strangers, or immigrants have for integration into European societies, or American Societies can be success, also known by many as "The American Dream, or the "European Success". It is true that there are Africans who make it. The list would be financial success, happiness, security, "La belle vie" and so forth. For others, or the majority, the prospects are difficulties dealing with the consequences of colonization including the harsh realities of discrimination, racism, rejection, and non-inclusion in the Universal Declaration of Human Rights as stated. For example, Article 13 of the Universal Declaration of Human Rights states that (1) Everyone has the right to freedom of movement and residence within the borders of each State. (2) Everyone has the right to leave any country, including his own, and return to his country.[31] The historical development of international human rights shows otherwise. Do Africans have the right to work in Europe, and in America, like other citizens of the world? "When governments, activists, or United Nation documents refer to "human rights" today they are almost certainly referring to the human rights recognized in international and national law rather than rights in a moral of philosophical sense"[32]. What rights do Africans have within Africa, or Europe, or America? It is interesting to find that the realities of remittance hold many of the answers as to how significant it is in the lives of millions of Africans.

According to the United Nation, *World Economic and Social Survey*, in developing countries, remittances are the most important source of external funding after corporate investments, and they amount to almost three times the value of donations through development assistance and charity. Many experts agree that there are more international migrants today than ever before, and their number is set to increase. Khalid Koser said that the relationship between migration and development is a complex and divisive issue: the subject of intense public and political concern, and the reality of many migrants—both legal and irregular—in one of exploitation and abuse. [33]

Several approaches to data gathering were used in this work, including historical and qualitative analysis, and semi-structured and open-ended interview. The usage of secondary data could be just as relevant.

Remittance to Senegal

- The Word Bank reported that Senegal is the 4th largest receiver of remittance in Africa in 2007.
- The Banque Africaine de Developpement reported that Senegal received 1.254 million euros in 2007
- Remittance from France (449 million euros).
- Remittance from Italy (350 million euros).
- Remittance from Spain (180 million euros).
- Remittance from USA (108 million euros).
- Remittance from Africa (99 million euros).
- Remittance from the rest of the word (69 million euros). [34]

Sociologically, politically and economically speaking, it is extremely important to understand both the culture and the economics behind remittance. As it was well said in Frantz Fanon's

---

31 Universal Declaration of Human Rights. The Human rights USA Steering Committee.
32 Clapham Andrew (2007) *Human Rights*. Oxford. University Press. Page 23.
33 Koser Khalid. (2007) *International Migration*. Oxford University Press. Page 43.
34 Etude BAD : « Les Transferts des fonds des migrants, un enjeu de développement ». Janvier 2008.

classic "A Dying Colonialism" that is a clear call for the West to recognize the dignity of the non-Western. One needs to have the scientist understanding of precolonial societies in Africa and Europe. Professor Cheikh Anta Diop stated: "The principal source of revenue for the sovereigns of Black Africa, from antiquity to modern times, from the Indian Ocean to the Atlantic, i.e., from the Nubia of Herodotus and Diotorus Sicalus to the Ghana of Bakri and the Mali of Ibn Buttuta and Khaldun and the Songhai of Sadi Kati, was gold extracted from mines."[35]

The culture behind the remittance is profound, just as profound as the culture of how to get the gold thru work, wherever work can be found, and by any means necessary. There was a culture in Africa before colonization. Kendall defines culture as knowledge, language, values, customs, and material objects that are passed from person to person and from one generation to the next in a human group or society. He asked the question where would we be without culture. How would we communicate? What rules would need to be followed to keep order and create patterns in a society?[36] Thus, it is important to understand how some important cultural elements have changed more quickly than others, disrupting the traditional cultural system in Africa, particularly between 1854 and 1960, a period known by the French as the "French Civilizing Mission".[37]

The crisis

More than half a century after independence, the Pan Africanists continue to view the colonization of the African continent as the greatest threat of contemporary Africa. The problem is not only limited to the leadership crisis, but more complex than that, a problem of global apartheid supported by the Word Bank, and the International Monetary Fund. Presently, most of the West African nations depend heavily on the remittance that African migrants must send regularly, and increasingly, to rescue the population. Paradoxically, more oil, gas, gold, zircon, and other valuable resources are being discovered, exploited and exported, while the jobless rate is increasing in West Africa. These new resources do not diminish the flow of migration, but seem to increase it.

Thousands of African men and women are dying trying to reach Europe or America, despite the discovery of gas in Mali, gold, bauxite, aluminum in Guinea and Ghana; Gaz and oil and zircon in Senegal. Senegal continuously faces more than 25 percent unemployment, and thousands of youngsters ready to migrate. How can West Africa retain the youth trying to cross the Sahara in their way to Europe? Field observations suggest that Senegalese violence is more often related to the social and economics of youth than to violence against women. What type of leadership is needed to decolonize or deconstruct the notion of helplessness and hopelessness of millions of Africans who still want to leave the continent?

35 Diop Cheikh Anta. (1987) *Precolonial Black Africa : A comparative Study of the Political and Social Systems of Europe and Black Africa, From Antiquity to the Formation of Modern States.* Lawrance Hill *105*

36 Watson Ron. (2005) The Spirit of Sociology. Pearson. 61

37 Ndao, El Hadi Ibrahima (2003) Senegal, Histoire des Conquetes Democratiques. Les Nouvelles Edition Africaines.

The French Civilizing Mission

To understand the history of African colonization, and recognize its impact thru the decolonization process, one must understand "The French Civilizing Mission." We will refer to this mission thru the important works of the great W.E.B. Dubois, Cheikh Anta Diop, Ali Mazrui, Amabou Mahtar M'bow, and Djibril Tamsir Niane. Their scientific publications and speeches also guided our understanding of facts about Africa's relationships with Europe and America. To various degrees, they all have important sociological and political approaches about Africa's struggle with both colonization and decolonization. The French colonization of Senegal began in 1659 in Walo which will become Saint-Louis du Senegal.[38] In 1764, the first mayor arrived in Senegal from France. His name was Charles Thevenot. The occupation became official with the formation of the four communes: Saint-Louis and Goree in 1872, Rufisque in 1880, and Dakar in 1887.

Christian missionaries played a significant role in promoting and shaping the advent of French colonialism, and they were direct active agents of European imperialism. Governor Louis Faidherbe quickly achieved many conquests by building up a highly discipline Senegalese army, locally recruited and trained in the use of the most up-to-date weaponry from Europe. It was this Senegalese army commanded largely by local Afro-French officers, which provided the French with their main frontline troops for the conquest of western Africa in the 1880s and 1890s. Between 1879 and 1881 the French began the most aggressive policy of widespread colonization in West Africa. Consequently, the French were able to dominate West Africa not only militarily, but politically and economically. There was no significant resistance from Senegal, Guinea, Mali, Dahomey, Niger, Chad, or any other colonies that could defeat the French colonizers. The French government formally took over the administration of French West Africa. Dramatic political changes prompted the exploitation of all the natural resources: Coffee, cacao, rice, millet, sugar, palm oil, gold, silver, diamond, bauxite, magnesium, aluminum, uranium, and so on- The Africans themselves produced the raw materials and the manufactured goods for exportation to Europe mainly. [39] [40]

The classic definition of colonialism is the process by which some nations enrich themselves through political and economic control of other nations. Diop explains why attempts of economic development and cooperation cannot succeed apart from the political unification of Black Africa. For colonization not to have succeeded, Diop would argue that shared common cultural heritage must have been preserved, and linguistic unification would have been a prerequisite. The French were never interested in multiculturalism. For them, recognizing a cultural diversity would have meant less power and an end to the colonialist system. The concept of cultural integration, meaning a close relationship among

---

38   Ndao, El Hadi Ibrahima (2003) Senegal, Histoire des Conquetes Democratiques. Les Nouvelles Edition Africaines.
39   Ndao, El Hadi Ibrahima (2003) Senegal, Histoire des Conquetes Democratiques. Les Nouvelles Edition Africaines.
40   J. Ki-Zerbo. General History of Africa. Methodology and African Prehistory. UNESCO. 1990. Page 5.

various elements of a cultural system turned out to be nothing but "assimilation" an empty rhetoric ---- walk, talk, eat, think, and speak like a French--- or else, you become a savage! Most anthropologists and ethnologists were definitely euro-centric.[41]

<hr/>

What is decolonization?

J.Ki-Zerbo and, Amadou Mohtar Mbow, both argued the meanings of anthropology and ethnology in their classic publication, *General History of Africa*: "For a long time these two disciplines were enlisted in the service of colonization and domination: by presenting African and other societies as primitive and backward, and by taking apart the mechanisms holding them together they made easier to administer them as dependent or, in other words, contributed to the development of underdevelopment." [42] The place of history in African society was in doubt in the literature until 1938. Thus, one would find it difficult to even acknowledge the existence of the concept of colonization, much less decolonization. Earlier authors on Africa, its peoples and their cultural history, never set foot in Africa. That changed. From 1945 onwards, the *Societe Africaine de Culture*, and its journal *Presence Africaine*, along with African intellectuals, trained in the techniques of historical method, which they used to their continents, restoring objectivity, and adding to the methodology intensive use of such resources as oral tradition, linguistics, and so on. [43]

The Great Cheikh Anta Diop argued that Egypt is to Black Africa what Greece and Rome is to the Occident. Diop's definition of colonialism was very different from Senghor's definition of colonialism. No intellectual has been able to explain the enormity of the difference better than W.E.B. Dubois. The formidable thing about Dubois and Diop was that they never shy away in explaining the brutality of colonialism. Interestingly enough, they both understood why economic development cannot succeed apart from political unification of black Africa. They both understood that the preservation and development of Africa's natural resources could transform the life of its people. And they also agreed that grouping and sharing common cultural heritage and linguistic unification are all possible. [44] These principles are different from the Eurocentric views that define colonialism as mission to civilize the African – and to teach them French grammar, and the French way a thinking, working, and praying, dressing, cooking, dancing, et la joie de vivre. The Pan-Africanists, on the other hand, view colonialism as a racist, political, economic, cultural, and military domination of one nation over another. They would argue the question of decolonization only if colonialism itself is properly defined.

41   Ndao, El Hadi Ibrahima (2003) Senegal, Histoire des Conquetes Democratiques. Les Nouvelles Edition Africaines.

42   J. Ki-Zerbo. General History of Africa. Methodology and African Prehistory. UNESCO. 1990. Page 5.

43   J. Ki-Zerbo. General History of Africa. Methodology and African Prehistory. UNESCO. 1990. Page 15.

44   Diop Cheikh Anta; Carlos Moore. Black Africa: The Economic and Cultural Basis for a Federated State. 1987.

African Strategy of Independence:

African social scientists have shied away from making serious policy analysis on how to go about total independence, much less building on valid and reliable policies for emergence. The Nigerian social scientist, Chinweizu stated that Africa's independence struggle has returned some measure of autonomy to African hands. But the winning of that autonomy left still unaccomplished our total liberation from Western political, economic, and cultural hegemony. It still leaves undone the construction of a revitalized African society. Chinweizu's central argument turns toward today's task. He said that if we wish to protect Africa from new and more deadly imperialisms, we must make of Africa a first-rate power. Our condition—past and present as well as future—demands that we impose that enterprise upon ourselves. But as we look about us, what is there to see? Just as slaving wrecked the polities of our past, neocolonial plunder is wrecking the polities we inherited at independence. Construction of an independent African power is a task we must speedily carry out if we want to avoid another loss of sovereignty. Chinweizu concluded by saying that in order to understand what exactly remains to be done, we have to examine critically what has already been done, we must examine the conquest and colonization we suffered, evaluate the "independence" we won, and judge the use we have so far made of it. [45]

Migration and decolonization connection: The case of Senegal:

Senegal has been at the center of the intellectual, and political discussion regarding colonization, decolonization, culture, "negritude", assimilation, and independence, and integration, for nearly a century. The perspectives of Leopold Sedar Senghor of Senegal, whom I met as a young student at the US Embassy in Washington DC in 1977, gave me a long held belief about the nuances about independence and decolonization. Thirty years later, I had the privilege to meet with President Abdoulaye Wade, when he attended the Colloquium on Migration which I organized in Senegal as a Fulbright Professor of Social Policy. This extraordinary event give me new perspectives about the notions of cultural assimilation, self-determination and the interconnection with the opportunities through migration.

The perspectives of Aime Cesaire of Martinique who, beginning in 1945, promoted self-determination without state sovereignty became controversial. "As politicians, public intellectuals, and poets, they struggled to transform imperial France into a democratic federation, with former colonies as autonomous members of a transcontinental polity. In so doing, they revitalized past but unrealized political projects and anticipated impossible futures by acting as if they had already arrived." [46] There were many

---

45 Chinweizu. The West and the Rest of Us. Vintage Books. 1975. Page 33.

46 Freedom Time: Negritude, Decolonization, and the Future of the World. A panel discussion with Garry Wilder, E Balibar Etienne, and Gayatri Chakravorty, moderated by Bachir Diagne. Columbia Maison Francaise, Institute of African Studies, and Institute of Comparative Literature and Society. Columbia Maison Francaise. Facebook.

weaknesses that made the decolonization process difficult. However, from Senghor's perspective, the problem lied within the context which he indicated as following:

> The weakness of the Nation is neither at the level of the highest state official nor at the level of the peasants of the Bush, nor even with the skilled worker; it is at the level of the lower and intermediary civil servants, many of whom are not yet decolonized, those who are not still aware of the fact that independence requires an increased effort of work, discipline and also politeness. [47]

The literature clearly indicates that Senghor, like Felix Houphouet-Boigny of Ivory Coast, repudiated the quest for national sovereignty, after they abandoned the populist militancy which defeated the French and the British. Senghor was the man to implement France's neocolonial strategy. In a speech at Strasbourg in 1950, Senghor said:

> ...in this world besieged with nuclear anxiety,...men if not people prefer liberties to Liberty; to the independence of each country the material and moral independence of each of their citizen...To speak of their independence is to reason with the head on the ground, and the feet in the air; it is not to reason at all. It is to advance a false problem. [48]

It is not clear to many if Senghor felt the quest for independence would alienate the colonial powers so much that the newly independent nation would be left without any allies in a hostile world – or that his concern was less security, more lack of faith in Africans to create a good civil society of their own.

It is impossible to deny that Senegal's colonial experience has profoundly affected its modern development. This fact has already been stressed by various scholars such as Sheldon Gellar, Samir Amin, Walter Rodney, and others. They have all examined what is called the "civilizing mission". The French colonialists defended their acquisition of colonies with the idea that they would bring peace, prosperity, and the benefit of French civilization to the "backward and primitive" people fortunate enough to come under French rule. It has also been well documented that the colonial situation permitted France to deny its colonial subject the political and civil rights that its own people enjoyed at home. Further, it allowed the French to make policy largely on the basis of what was good for France and for French nationals living in the colonies. Therefore, due to political, economic, and cultural domination, forcibly imposed by the French continues to have tremendous impact in Senegal, in the "post-colonial era". [49] [50] [51]

47 Markovitz Irving. Leopold Sedar Senghor and the Politics of Negritude, New York, Atheneum. 1969, p.11.
48 Chin Weizu The West and the Rest of Us. 1975. Vintage books. P.97.
49 Gellar, Sheldon. Senegal: An African Nation between Islam and the West. London, England: west View Press, 1982.
50 Rodney, Walter. How Europe Underdeveloped Africa. Washington D.C.: Howard University Press, 1982.
51 Seck, Magueye. Alcohol Use In Harmony And In Contradiction With Cultural Norms in Senegal. Boston: University of Massachusetts, Boston. 1987.

Migration racism and xenophobia

The literature has neglected the topic of migration in Senegal and specifically with regard to women. However, recently, Senegalese sociologists have taken the challenge to investigate and publish in this topic in an unprecedented way, (Tandian, 2006; Coulibaly, 2007; Sow, 2007; Tall, 2010). Another aspect that has been overlooked in the literature in the intersect between migration and youth and health, although it is generally understood that health status is a critical variable for young people particularly when they migrate. According to UNESCO, at its 175th session, the Executive Board noted that the contemporary African migration is a matter of international concern that requires concerted action and fits into UNESCO's priority targets Africa, youth, and least developed countries. [52]

The document added that the issue of youth migration stresses the human rights implications of this phenomenon. Social scientists have argued that Africa is a continent characterized by long-standing and intensive migration practices. There exists some documentation on cross-border movement, for trade-related opportunities since colonial times. The literature also indicates that the creation of post-independence nation-states affected these processes, obscuring the distinction between internal and international movements. The total number of migrants in Africa thus rose from 9 million in 1960 to 16 million in 2000, with Western Africa hosting the largest share of these migrants (42 per cent), followed by Eastern Africa (28 percent) and Southern Africa (12 per cent). It is estimated that 5 million African migrants live in Europe. (UNESCO, 2007, P.2).

A recent history has highlighted tensions between the African migrants and the European countries. Mass expulsions or deportations fed by racism and xenophobia toward African migrants are now frequent. The Africans on the move include unprecedented number of women. There are many categories which sociologists now use to describe these migrants: Farm laborers, seasonal migrants, unskilled workers and nomads, clandestine workers, professionals, traders, refugees, and cross-border workers. (U.N. Global Commission on International Migration). [53]

"My crime is working without documentation"

The responses I gathered from the Senegalese migrants validate the same notions in the literature. They have been overwhelming. "If I don't send money, my family will starve!". "I will do any work to earn money". "I cannot afford to return to Senegal—to do what?" "It is sad that people back home do not understand the conditions under which we are living in Europe". "I have no saving, and I am sick, and I must work". "I am in and out of prison all the time—my crime is working without documentation—and at this point I don't give a f---!" "We came here

---

52 Tandian Aly. 2008. « Barca ou Barsaax « Allez a Barcelone ou Mourir : Le désenchantement des familles et des Candidats a la migration. Diasporas, Histoire et Societe, no9, pp.124-137.

53 http://www.irinnews.org/report.asp?ReportID=53633&SelectRegion=West_Africa

believing that everything is taken care of—that we came to Spain legally". This last quote was from a group of 25 girls, and who all had visas for farming. They did not understand the contracts they signed; nobody in the group did because they did not understand Spanish. They had been used and abused since they arrived to Spain—many run away, many got sick because of the agricultural products they used in the farms. Very few stayed. Many went to cities like Valencia to work as housekeepers, and some became sex workers." "The police violence and the racism—just getting harder and harder". "There is literally no place to go for support". "The prisons are full of migrants—it is mind boggling what is going on!" "I don't know what is going on—I am desperate! "I got scared, when I see people who get sick and died, because they are afraid to go the hospital." "Our crime is working without documentation".

◇◇

Decolonization and Emergence

The past few years, the concept "Emergence" is being used by politicians and academicians all over the African continent. But, what is emergence? Who coined this term? Why is it necessary to link emergence to colonization or decolonization? Some refer to emergence to promote markets and democracy globally, while others refer to emergence for developing local markets. Some would refer to emergence when they advocate for jobs, education, health care; giving poor people property, and land reform. Recently, there are movements pushing for the development of a system of currency independent from the French monetary system. Throughout history, money has taken a variety of forms – shells, strips of leather, cloth, event livestock were used as early system of currency. The development of a system of currency was in the past one of the key indicators of an empire's influence, power, and self-sustainability.[54] For many Africans the concept of emergence remains not only unclear but unmeasurable in most instances.

In Indonesia, the Chinese Indonesian community makes up 3% of the population but control 70% of the economy. In Philippines, the Chinese Filipino community is 1% of the population but controls 60% of the economy with a result being resentment on the part of the Chinese minority creating an ethnic conflict. [55] Similar situations occurred in Nigeria, Kenya, South Africa and many other African states. Will West Africa in its new quest for emergence also suffer "Ethnic market-dominant minority" or "Global market-dominant minority"? What else beside the remittance phenomenon is awaiting? Some groups inherited market dominance because of colonial legacies like apartheid, and in other cases, it may be due to the culture and family networks of these groups. For many groups there is no clear single explanation. [56]

---

54 International Monetary Fund, and the World Economic Outlook.
55 Chua, Amy (2002). World on Fire. Doubleday.
56 Chua, Amy (2002). World on Fire. Doubleday.

Sociocultural and Political Context of Emergence: The case of Senegal

The population of Senegal is estimated at 15.4 million, in 2016, with an annual growth rate of 6.6 percent. Senegal is made up of over twenty ethnic groups, the largest being Wolof/Lebous (40.8%) followed by the Pulars (27.6%), Serers (14.4%), Diolas (5.3%) and a structure that had been in place prior to independence. In 1982, Senegal joined The Gambia to form the short-lived confederation of the Senegambia, but the merger failed and in 1989 the union was dissolved. Present day Senegal is divided into 14 regions, 113 municipalities, 370 rural communities and 14,400 villages. The first President, Leopold Sedar Senghor, ruled from 1960 to 1980, and handed over the power peacefully to Abdou Diouf. In 2000 Senegal witnessed the first truly contested election which resulted in democratic political transition with the Senegalese Democratic Party (PDS) and Abdoulaye Wade winning over the traditional Socialist Party (PS) of Leopold Sedar Senghor and Abdou Diouf. Senegal is one of the most stable countries in Africa.

However, the Casamance region has, for the last 30 years, been under-going Africa's longest low-intensity conflict, causing hundreds of deaths and injuries. Peace in Casamance is imperative for emergence in Senegal. The conflict in Casamance has cut agricultural production by 50%. The tourist industry has also been devastated by the conflict, with many of the industry's 16,000 employees being dismissed because of their continuing struggle.

[57] The newly-elected President, Macky Sall, former Prime Minister of Senegal, has stressed that resolving the Casamance crisis is a top priority.

In Senegal, one must acknowledge that the civil society played an extremely important role in bringing about political change in 2012. Youth movements, the M23 movement and the *Y-en-a Marre*, were vocal about the deteriorating governance environment as well as the need to respect the constitution and the democratic transition process. In June 2011, an attempt by the current government to modify the constitution, allowing victory in presidential election with only 25 percent of vote, was rejected by the Legislature after strong resistance from the population, thus demonstrating the resilience of civil society. [58] These Movements built on the 2011 "Assises Nationales du Senegal" led by the great Amadou-Mahtar M'bow, former Director-general of Unesco, who stated "For a long time, all kind of myths and prejudices concealed the true history of Africa from the world at large. As a leader, he was able to deal with the lack of written sources and document for Africa more effectively than any previous leader in history. He was able to help explain precisely critical elements of colonization, neo-colonization and decolonization thru the series the "General History of Africa." His contribution had made it possible for scholars to continue the important work on cultural integration and the link with the colonial system.

---

57 The Word Bank. International Development Association; International Finance Corporation Report. Africa Region. (FY2013-2017).

58 The Word Bank. International Development Association; International Finance Corporation Report. Africa Region. (FY2013-2017).

Cultural Integration

Cultural integration is defined by sociologists as the close relationship among various elements of a cultural system. It is very important to mention some facts about Senegal before the arrival of the French. Senegal was a kingdom for many centuries, with five independent provinces: Walo, Cayor, Baol, Sine, and Saloum. These provinces were politically and economically independent from each other. There was clearly mutual respect between those provinces. They had very similar economic systems based on agriculture, hunting, fishing, and trading. The Wolof were and still are the largest ethnic group. The Wolof lived everywhere with any other group in the territory. The other groups are Toucouleur who became Muslims in early 1800; the Serers mostly converted to Christianity by the French missionaries; and the Diola, mostly animists. Before the arrival of Islam and Christianity in Senegal, there were common elements dominated by the Tieddo tradition and religion which included beliefs in intermediary spirits, sacrifices, witches, fertility rites, and magic.[59]

Interestingly, the use of cloth as money, according to anthropologists, was the means of exchange, which was introduced by the Wolof long before the European arrived. Women used to card locally grown cotton and spin the thread. Wolof men from the slave class wove the cloth on a typical narrow West African loom in strips about five inches wide. Several of these strips sewn together were called "malan" in Wolof or "pagne" in French. These strips were used in exchange for goods, rice, corn, oil, land, or anything except alcoholic beverages. Alcohol consumption was controlled by ritual, rather than commodity exchanges. Palm trees were the major sources of alcohol production in the kingdom. [60] [61] The French decimated the palm trees in Senegal, and replaced the palm wine with their own imported wine from "Bordeau, France".

Senghor's argument about a weak nation, and what constitutes dependency and independence much less decolonization, remains bewildering for many, even half century later. The contradictions in his statement about the weakness of the nation not being situated at the highest level of state officials are quite apparent now. It is also clear that the decolonization process is a top down process. This process can never be a bottom up process simply because the poor peasants suffer the loss of their freedom because they had been forced to assimilate values that were and are still incompatible with their traditional values. Yes, Senghor did compromise with the colonialists, and the religious leaders, but at whose best interest? He blamed the intermediary civil servants, whom he said are not yet decolonized, as if he and the elites of that period were decolonized. Then, he insulted the Africans when he said that "… independence requires an increased effort of work, discipline and politeness."

---

59 Kurian, Thomas. Encyclopedia of the Third World. Volume III. New York. Facts on File, Inc., 1982.

60 Seck, Magueye. *Alcohol Use In Harmony And In Contradiction With Cultural Norms in Senegal*. Boston: University of Massachusetts, Boston. 1987.

61 Ames, David Wason. *Continuity and Change in African Culture*. Chicago: University Press. 1959.

Independence, Peace and Service

Senegal also has a very long history of resistance against colonization. Sheikh Ahmadou Bamba, the founder of the Sufi Path Muridiyya and the spiritual school Khidmatul Khadim, the School of Peace and Service had resisted the French domination and colonization from religious, social, and political grounds. The French attempted to use their power and their colonial authority against Bamba and failed miserably each time. They exiled him twice out of Senegal, still could not defeat him. Sheikh Ahmadou Bamba lived from 1853 to 1927 while Senegal was under French colonial rule. Sheikh Ahmadou Bamba was committed to the revival of authentic Islam, the religion of Peace and his only ideal was to serve humanity by giving teachings in accordance with the prophetic model. He devoted his entire life to awakening human consciousness, both among the oppressed and the oppressors.[62]

Since his early childhood, he renounced all worldly things. At the death of his father he was offered the post of counsellor to the king but he declined the offer. Sheikh Ahmadou Bamba was perceived by the French colonizers as a threat and was therefore subjected to a multitude of ordeals by the colonizers who wanted to eliminate him. However, Sheikh Ahmadou Bamba never surrendered to the colonizers. Rather he persevered in his mission as a conscience awakener for both oppressors and oppressed. This approach appalled the colonial authorities which soon decided to arrest and banish him. He was exiled in Gabon from 1895 to 1902 and in Mauritania from 1903 to 1907. Despite the harshness of the conditions in which he was exiled, he bore no ill feelings for the colonizers. Rather, his non violent approach led him to seek to liberate the oppressors from their violence and the oppressed from the misery of their condition as victims.

Since Sheikh Ahmadou Bamba considered God as the sole authority and the only will power that reigned, he never blamed the colonisers for his condition. On the contrary he saw God's hand in all these trials and accepted them as a path of spiritual elevation specially traced for him. Thus he was devoid of all hatred, resentment and any form of rancour towards the colonisers. Towards the latter part of his life, France decided to thank Sheikh Ahmadou Bamba for his conciliatory and peaceful attitude by awarding him the title of Legion d'Honneur. However, the Sheikh declined the title, saying that his good deeds were meant for the pleasure of God and hence he only expected rewards from the Almighty.

Khidmatul Khadim, School of Peace and Service

Sheikh Ahmadou Bamba hoped to establish a model society based on peace, where it is possible for every human being to live in peace and harmony with his neighbours and with the Creator of the Universe, irrespective of differences. The thought and action of Sheikh Ahmadou Bamba can be seen to consist of several characteristic stages which represent the pre-requisites for the

---

62   http://www.international-sufi-school.org/cab_thought_en.html

making of a peacemaker and an agent of service in society.

In contrast to the French civilization ideal of *Liberte, Egalite, Fraternite*, he proposed the ideals of choice, liberty, and love, and service to community: the concept of Khidma.

Service to Humanity: The Concept of Khidma

Humanity constitutes a unique family which is taken care of by God. He who is most loved by God is the one who makes himself most useful to this family of God. The approach of Sheikh Ahmadou Bamba : the building of an equitable society geared towards peace In order to actualize his approach of non-violence, Sheikh Ahmadou Bamba strived, against all odds, towards the building of an equitable social model geared towards peace. This model, where the human being is at the very center, provides the conditions for the development of the human being at all levels so that he can live up to his full potential and fully assume his role of vicegerent of God on earth.

This model is illustrated by the Peace City of Touba, a city recognized as Model Peace City by the United Nations Human Settlement Division in 1996. This social model is one that satisfies the following four essential requirements: clothing, shelter, food, peace. The realization of such a model was only possible through the commitment of Sheikh Ahmadou Bamba to an ideal of service to humanity[63]

Dependency cannot be viewed as simply an external phenomenon; it has both cultural and political impacts. Leading theorists define dependence as a conditioning situation, in which the economies of one group of countries are conditioned by the development and expansion of others.[64] Among these theorists, the great W.E.B. Dubois. Dubois was the founding father of the Pan-Africanist Perspective. He was the first African American to earn a doctoral degree from Harvard, and became one of the greatest sociologists of our time, author of the most comprehensive and classic publication in sociology of health "The Philadelphia Negro". Dr. Dubois wrote about poverty, hardship, and diseases plaguing the African continent from a unique and impressive perspective (Agbeyebiawo, 1998). In June, 1947, at the 38th annual conference of the NAACP, Dr. Dubois talked about how wrongly world controlling bodies perceived poverty. He stated:

> *Most intelligent people today, even in civilized parts of the earth believe that it is normal and necessary that most human beings should not have enough to eat and wear and insufficient shelter; and because of this inevitable poverty, most human beings must be ignorant, diseased and to a large extent criminal. The persons who believe this mythical witchcraft are ignorant of the plain teaching of science and industrial techniques especially in the nineteenth and twentieth centuries."* [65]

---

63   http://www.international-sufi-school.org/cab_thought_en.html
64   Rodney, Walter. *How Europe* Underdeveloped *Africa*. Washington D.C.: Howard University Press, 1982.
65   Agbeyebiawo Daniel (2000) The life and Woks of W.E.B. Dubois. Accra, Ghana.

According to Dr. Dubois, social behavior must be understood as a result of certain social conditions and institutional dynamics. Race matters for him. Race is a social construction, involving matters of economics, history, politics, heritage, and culture, much more than simple biology and physicality. Racial distinctions and racial constructs are supremely important and crucially central to how human beings experience the world, from health to wealth, from literacy to religion, from crime to politics, from city governance to international relations. More than any sociologist, past and present, the literature shows Dr. Dubois as the leading voice explaining how health in Africa is directly linked to the colonial theory. This is the theory that argues that race is used by dominant group in society to oppress the Africans. He equally articulated the nativism theory where he argued against the hostility toward immigrants and efforts to restrict their rights.

Dubois was a fierce fighter against the believers of cultural deficiency theories, and the theories of social pathology. Instead, Dr. Dubois urged African to unite. He argued:

> If Africa unites it will be because each part, each nation, each tribe gives up a part of its heritage for the good of the whole. That is what union means; that is what Pan-Africa means: When a child is born into the tribe the price of his growing up is to give over a part of his freedom to the tribe. <u>This is soon learns or dies.</u> When tribe becomes a union of tribes, the individual tribes surrenders some part of its freedom to the paramount tribe.[66]

How racial dynamic is linked with class dynamic, and how society is separated are critically analyzed in the Dubois perspective.

Racial distinctions and racial constructs

Racial distinctions and racial constructs are supremely important and crucially central to how human beings experience the world, from health to wealth, from literacy to religion, from crime to politics, from city governance to international relations.[67] Since the days of the European partition and conquest of the 28 million square kilometers of Africa, the central questions of "overproduction, surplus capital, and under-consumption in industrial nations" have not been clearly analyzed in their impact in neocolonial Africa. In other words, many African nationalists and anti-colonial movements would recognize that since the 1880s, considerably little had taken place to free the continent from a well-coordinated stratification, politically partitioned, and systematically occupied continent. [68] Although many African leaders and their followers fought harshly for the liberation of the continent, the concept of decolonization itself remains a myth for many.

66 Agbeyebiawo Daniel (2000) The life and Woks of W.E.B. Dubois. Accra, Ghana.
67 Zuckerman Phil. 2004. *The Social Theory of W.E.B. Dubois.* Pine Forge Press.
68 Boahen A, Adu. 1990. *General History of Africa.* UNESCO. Page 10.

Conclusion

Cheikh Anta Diop's argument that attempts at economic development and cooperation cannot succeed apart from the political unification of Black Africa is still valid.[69] The process by which France and England, and other developed countries continue to enrich themselves through political and economic control of the African nations is increasingly being challenged. Corruption among the African leaders whose objectives also help maintain the colonial policies are being challenged across Africa. The reality being that the colonizers still have control over the African leadership just the way it was more than a century ago.

More African leaders are becoming aware that having a primary concern for the well-beings of the African people is becoming more effective in moving toward decolonization. Conversely, the instrumental African leaders, group leaders that focusses on the completion of tasks dictated by the Western nations, and keeping the neocolonial policies in place, now realize that ending of colonization, and poverty, and suffering, will be difficult to achieve. In other words, ending the politically partitioned continent, and dismantling its well-coordinated stratification is paramount. The economic devastation will not end when it is designed to serve the interest of the colonizers and the African leaders who support them.

Obviously, the poor suffer more shocks that the non-poor and have fewer or no coping strategies due to the absence of an effective safety net system. Many of these poor ends up migrating. It is alarming when the World Bank acknowledges that unsustainable management of natural resources, primarily for food production as well as for food energy, hunting and gathering. Terrestrial and oceanic ecosystems are at risk, with land degradation affecting 34 percent of the land area, causing deforestation (0.5%) and overfishing, and contributes to increased poverty. The level of food insecurity for 28percent of the population is extremely high.[70] Equally alarming is that the African leadership has not yet solved the need for an African solidarity which has become politically, economically, and sociologically imperative for a decolonization, liberation, and emerging Africa! The tasks can be reoriented toward this end, pushing for African solidarity, and unity. African solidarity is possible! Linguistic unification is possible; and the preservation and development of Africa's natural resources could transform the life of its people as Cheikh Anta Diop had already demonstrated fifty years ago.[71]

In addition to the leadership crisis which causes a major barrier against decolonization, this article also showed that the current immigration crisis as dangerous undertaking that weakens the culture and the development for Africa. In addition, this article revealed that there is a connection between the African mass migration to Europe and the failed attempt for decolonization. Massive poverty and unsustainable management of African resources point to widespread collusion between the colonizers

---

69   Diop Cheikh Anta. 19974. The Economic and Cultural Basis for a Federated State.
70   World Bank. 2013. Country Partnership Strategy For The Republic of Senegal. P.4.
71   Diop Cheikh Anta. 19974. The Economic and Cultural Basis for a Federated State.

and the corrupt African leadership. The millions of Africans who depart for Europe and America continue to empower both Europe and America, and impoverish Africa in a very significant way.

African nations depend heavily on remittance. However, the remittance that these migrants send to Africa cannot replace the human capital loss for Africa, nor solve the brain drain crisis. The social dysfunction this migration creates in Africa, the family breakup it causes, the lack of respect and lack of dignity, and the suffering, and alienation, discrimination, racism, and violence they face must be acknowledged and dealt with adequately. These variables are often not considered significant for the colonizers and their supporters who believe that the Africans are lethargic. These migrants are not lethargic, but only recently their stories are being disseminated. Thanks to their work and their remittance, poverty and the social indicators such as health and education, life expectancy and infant mortality would have been even more catastrophic in the African continent. Therefore, the African migrants and the Diasporas have become the counterforce to the process by which Europe enrich itself through political and economic control of Africa.

The reasons why leading economies, emerging empire and settler societies are no longer welcoming to Africans are numerous. Racism came as the primary cause. These nations want to their fill labor shortages, boost population growth, and stimulate business and trade, but without any respect to human rights. They want to continue to fulfill these goals without any sense of justice, civility or dialogue with the Africans. The mistreatment of African immigrants and African of the Diasporas is deeply rooted to slavery and

colonization; but also to the lack of solidarity among the Africa leaders. What is the best strategy for African to fight racism? This article argues that African solidarity must be the counterforce. This article forcefully states that corrupt leadership will add to the continental deficit, and the abandonment and abuse of workers in Africa, and the weakening of African workers in the Diaspora.

The decolonization of the mind is strategically critical. Fortunately, younger generation seems to understand the urgency of ending colonization. This phenomenon could be explained thru education, and the power of modern day communication such as the social media. The African youths are asking pertinent questions and demanding fundamental and well informed changes, as well human rights and social justice. These encouraging changes could provide more dialogue globally to deal with the inequities and injustices the Africans have been enduring for the past 400 years. The African youths must continue to share a common cultural heritage, and work toward the preservation and development of Africa's natural resources, and the creation of job opportunity.

Finally, peace and security will emerge with a decolonized Africa which will require not only the unity and the restoration of the historical consciousness of Africans, but a complete recovery of Africa's political sovereignty. The facts remain the same, after many decades, the Western industry still relies greatly on a wide range of strategic minerals from Africa. The great proportion of minerals extracted from Africa is for Western industry—very little is for Africa's industrialization. In terms of reserves, Africa has 90 percent of the world's cobalt, and over 80 percent of the world reserve of chrome, and more than 50 percent of the reserve of gold, and platinum.[72] These are just some of the strategic industrial minerals. Africa is emerging. Africa cannot afford to wait for the participants of Berlin to be convicted for the partition of Africa, nor can Africa wait for the next chapter of the French mission of civilization. The racism and imperialism cannot be undone by any **one** African nation. Solidarity among African and from the rest of the world is needed.

---

72 Mazrui, Ali. *The Africans: A triple Heritage.* Little Brown. Boston.

Chapter 4

Africa; The Music

African music is best defined by music created and performed by Africans. African music is the sonic expression of people of African descent. It is as rich melodically, profound rhythmically, varied harmonically, complex in its simplicity, and unimaginably textured as it reflects the immense diversity of its population groups and the depths of their cultural aesthetics but one thing is clear, from one side of the continent to another, the music always swings…

While regional African music is defined by its melodic colors, complex harmonic and tonal references, its foundations are in its rhythmic pulse. That notion of pulse, this feel so special that the Great African American composer Duke Ellington termed "Swing" in his composition "It Don't Mean A Thing if It Ain't Got that Swing", is central to all African music for it gives it, its identity, its life, its pulse, its groove, its flow and its reason to exist regardless of it region of origin…

Africans throughout the continent experience a culture of rhythm so powerful, so intense and so profound that it anchors and permeates all of their activities. Whether they walk or talk, work or create, argue or move, a notion of pulse is always central to that expression. That pulse is a reflection of a ternary appreciation of time. Ternary appreciation of time means that there is a deeply intuitive expression of a subdivision of time in three against two or 6 against four or eight from which the concept of swing or pulse emanates.

Whether they dance or talk, work or create, people of African descent swing regardless of their geographical locations. That ternary appreciation of time is central to an African sense of identity, for that subdivision of time is reflected in the movement that implies its rhythm and its nature, whether on the continent or in the Diaspora… Wherever Africans go… Africa goes…and so does its swing…

In the early 1940s, the West African scholar Leopold Sedar Senghor from Senegal defined this notion of rhythmic pulse that animated the activities and creativity as central to the expression of people of African descent as "rhythmic intuition" (Senghor 1964). This Senghorian doctrine of "rhythmic intuition" complemented and cemented academically the word and concept of "Negritude" which described in one word "the assembly of the cultural values of people of African descent" coined by Caribbean scholar Aime Cesaire (Cesaire 1935)[73].

While there is great diversity in the music of the African continent there is also great cultural affinity and identity as defined by

73   Cesaire, Aime. *L'Etudiant Noir.* Journal #3, May-June, 1935.

the use of the regional instruments created by these populations. Throughout the continent these cultural and musical influences cross the artificial borders established by the Berlin Conference of 1884 as ancestral populations groups found themselves separated and partitioned on each side of a different country i.e. Senegal & Gambia etc...

Africa is best understood culturally and musically when appreciated through the prism of five general geographical and cultural sections; the West from Nigeria to Senegal, the North from Morocco to Egypt, the East from Ethiopia to Tanzania, the South from Mozambique, South Africa, Botswana, Namibia and its Center from Angola, Congo, Cameroon and the Central African Republic.

In the Western part of the continent the instruments such as the Kora (21 string harp like), the Ngoni or Xalam (ancestor of the banjo celebrated in Nashville, TN), the Balafon (ancestor of the xylophone or marimba) and the various drums such as Sabar, Bougarabou, Djembes, Talking Drums etc... give the music its specific textural and aesthetic traits that are recognizably West Africans.

▲ *Ngoni*

Kora ▶

▲ *Balafon*

▲ *Sabar*

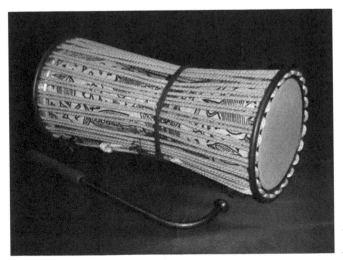

◀ *Talking Drums*

▲ *Djembes*

The Northern part of the continent is defined by a musical culture associated with the Malian string instrument called ngoni which became the Moroccan Sintir or Guimbri, several types of :lutes such as the Nay, and further to the north east the Nubian/Sudanese string instrument called the "Ould" (ancestor of the European lute), which became the favored instrument of Tunisian, and Egyptian cultures.

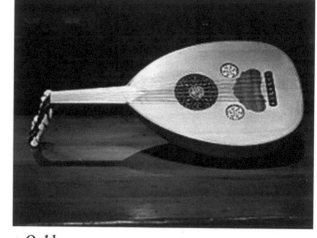

▲ *Ould*

◄ *Guimbri*

▼ *Sintir*

Nay ▶

The Eastern part of the continent is dominated by the culture of a string instrument i.e. the Kenyan "Niattiti" which we find depicted in the paintings and sculptures of Greek Antiquity i.e. (the Lyre). The spiritual instrument of the Ethiopian Church i.e. the "Begena" multi string harp like instrument, and the many rain forests sounding instruments of the Great Lakes regions of Eastern Africa such as the Kalimba or Thumb Piano coupled with a great culture of a cappella vocals. It is worth noting that the Eastern seaboard of the continent also benefited from the cultural influences of the Arabic Peninsula, India and China as their long lasting commercial exchanges established over centuries helped create a culture of its own through a process of cross cultural fertilization known as the Swahili coast. (Swahili being an Arabic term for coast).

Kalimba – ▶
Thumb Piano

◀ *Begena*

▼ *Niattiti*

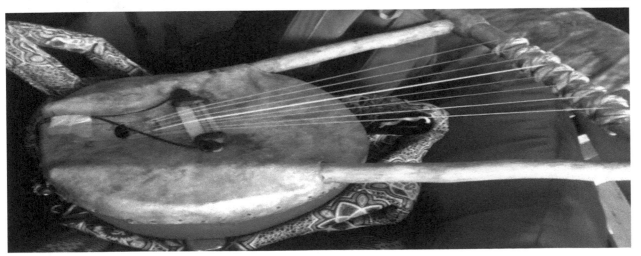

The Southern region of the continent also shows a commonality of Kalimba like instruments such as the Mbira or Thumb Piano of the Shona people of Zimbabwe that define a great sense of organized melodic and harmonic concepts with great clarity and intonation and an exciting culture of polyrhythmic drum patterns and Balafon like instruments. The very rich tradition of a cappella vocal present in Zulu culture confirms an elaborate culture of rhythmic and harmonization unique to that part of the world.

▲ *Marimba*

▼ *Ramkie Guitar*

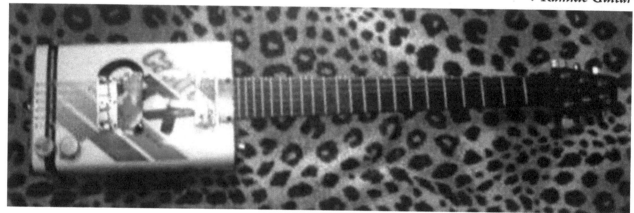

The Central part of the continent from Angola to the Congos displays a great variety of stylized vocals and intonations as different as its ethnic groups ranging from the BaAka people of the Equatorial forest making music with water to the various reeds and xylophone like instruments of the Bantus and Kongo people of that part of the world.

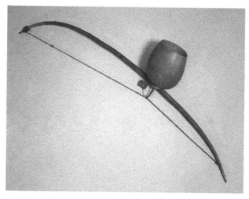

▲ *Umuduri*

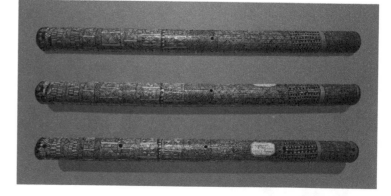

Nose Flute ▲

Africa, being the continent where Humanity began logically intimates that all of Humanity's music and musical concepts began in Africa. As African populations migrated out of Africa and began their defining respective journeys which directions will later define their respective anthropologies, shape their morphologies as an evolutionary response to their new geographical and climatic landscapes, from their African roots, new cultures emerge around the world.

It is clear that given that Humanity began approximately 4 million years ago, coupled with the fact that we have a scientifically conceptualized appreciation of modern Humans evolving at the 200,000 years BC mark, and that we have assessed the beginning of civilizations somewhere around 10,000 years BC, our educational system as presently distilled has not allowed our human brain the ability to begin appreciating the span of the horizon time period of our human evolutionary process, thus out of our general ignorance and fears is born a psychological need for cultural and political adherence to the very limited concept of race, when the reality is that there is only one race i.e. the Human race in all of its diversity. While the accepted scientific concept of One race is not a new theory, its teaching does not serve the immediate interests of those who benefit from the short sided politics of division and race mongering thus promulgating the intensification of the centrifugal energy born out of ignorance dispensing dissension for the purpose of seizing power.

We should note that Humans are only concerned with race because they can see. While the gift of eyesight is one of the defining joys of our ability to live as humans, it is also one of the major obstacles in our ability to learn profoundly and reflect intuitively. The conversation about the role of music, society and knowledge is a conversation at the complex intersection of the synergetic and dynamic forces of intuition, intuitive knowledge, Cartesian logic and creativity all of which require humans to close their eyes when immersed in the deep process of introspective truth seeking expressed through the ability to create, compose or improvise.

Although Africa and Africans have disseminated the concepts of music and some of its tonal canons to the rest of the world, Africa has also received the cultural gifts resulting in the journeys of its out of Africa migrating populations who have in turn created throughout the world an amazing and dizzying mosaic of varied cultures, societies, music and sounds.

In more contemporary times, Africans have also been very adept at selecting outside cultural influences and absorbing them into the creation of something new yet always remaining connected to their melodic and rhythmic African roots. That is why wherever Africans went, Africa went and its music always carried inflecting blue notes and swung rhythmically regardless of the destination of its populations.

Whether in the Blues and Rhythm & Blues, Bluegrass of the Appalachia, Gospel, Funk, or Jazz of North America, or the Sambas of Brazil, Rumbas of Cuba, Calypsos of the Caribbean, Soukous of Zaire importing elements of Cuban Rumbas, Reggae of Jamaica, Beguine and Zouk of Martinique and Guadeloupe, Compas of Haiti etc… African music always swings…

To those who will begin arguing about the length of the book or whatever else may be missing in its chapters, kindly let me re-state that the continent of Africa is too ancient in its geology and anthropology, too rich in history and historical markers that we continue to unearth daily, too complex scientifically, and humanly therefore culturally to be addressed in one book and as such this book does not pretend to do so. It is simply the first edition of an attempt to give the readers an African perspective and understanding of the cultural dynamics and its connections to our common human ancestry, history and to begin signaling some of the contemporary political dynamics that have shaped its music because as I have said many times…Music is an expression of cultural power… African music represents in its seeming simplicity the refinement of an enormous complexity and from the depth of its complexity a summary in its genial simplicity…in other words, "not everybody can swing"… African music's complexity is masked by a seeming simplicity…that one only discovers when he/she attempts to perform it…and/or try to swing…

Before we begin looking at the five regions of Africa and their musical sonic landscape we should have a conversation about the seminally important Malian Ngoni or Banjo and its role in disseminating West African cultural aesthetic markers that will forever shape and provide the foundation for the music of North America through the rural Blues, Blues, Gospel, Jazz, Rhythm & Blues and Soul…

Today in academia we know this much…this literature review surveyed the academic information referring to the role of the banjo as a vector for the aesthetics of the music of the Malinke people of the medieval Empire of Mali, West Africa (10th-14th century) in ethnic identity formation in the Diaspora specifically concerned with the Southern Plantations of the nascent colonial American period and the cultural contributions of West Africans brought during the Atlantic Slave Trade period of the 17th-19th century.

The context of this literature review aims at clarifying the purposely left nebulous academic information that addresses the immense impact of the musical culture of the Malinke people of West Africa, who are the creators of several string instruments including the banjo, and have a rich and very evolved set of musical aesthetics that anchor the music of most populations in West Africa who came under the cultural, economic and military rules of the medieval Empire of Mali from the 10th to the 14th century and what that West African culture brought to the American shores during the period of the Atlantic Slave Trade from the 16th century to the end of the 19th century and contributed to the music of America's musical capital Nashville through the use of its original instrument i.e. the banjo, its tonalities, rhythmic patterns, and Blues melodic contours and inflections.

There is ample academic information about the provenance of the banjo and significant information about the African character of the instrument and its aesthetics but that information has been left scattered thus, most Africans and African Americans have been left without a clear sense of cultural heritage and are not able to assess the cultural and musical value of the banjo as an instrument and its role as an umbilical cord to their own West African culture in the process of the making of their cultural identity formation in the North American diaspora. This academic endeavor is an attempt to connect the dots to address logically the academic references that should have long ago connected the music and the culture of the second medieval empire of West Africa i.e. the Empire of Mali (10th-14th) to the foundation of the early aesthetics of American music as brought over by West Africans during the Slave Trade. This literature review sheds some light both on the provenance of the instrument as well as that of the culture from which it emanates but first we must have an appreciation for why there is an academic fog in the world of ethnomusicology when it comes to connecting the dots from West African culture to the nascent culture of Africans in North America in the Southern plantations of the North American colonies. Before proceeding, we must frame our quest with the following statement from the eminent Malian guitarist/vocalist Ali Farka Toure who stated that "in Anthropology there isn't such a thing as Black Americans but there are Blacks in America...which means that... they came with their Culture". This statement defines the direction of our academic quest for the aesthetic cultural markers of West Africa who will define North American culture and aesthetics forever through the Blues.

We begin with Ghanaian Oxford professor Kofi Agawu's work entitled "Representing African Music" (2003)[74] which stimulated the academic debate by addressing some concerning Western academic and socio-cultural shortcomings by pointing out that Western scholars were mostly responsible for the written scholarship about Africa and its music. The questions had to do with the socio-cultural and analytical processes and tools Western musicologists and later on, ethnomusicologists used to qualify music and culture when they were not culturally issued from any of them or even spoke the languages of any of them, let alone being able to demonstrate a level of proficiency in the instrumental expression of such African music and rhythms by their own admissions. What qualifications did such Western foreigners to the ancient culture of Africa possessed that would allow them to issue academic proclamations about an African culture they were

trying to analyze, yet knew very little about and how reliable and valid such academic observations were within the context of the colonial mentalities and vocabulary of the times? As we have said before, most of what has been written about African music has not been written by Africans issued from such communities therein lies the debate as to how much academic validity and reliability such Western academic renderings carry. Given the academic historicity of the vagaries of the colonial and post-colonial periods which were marred by the racial prejudices of the times that led Christian scholar Paul Hiebert (1987)[75] to caution thinkers, scholars, and the Christian clergy as a whole about the importance of re-thinking the inherent biases that may have colored their scholarship of yesteryears in his eponymous work entitled "Transformative Worldviews" (1987), a non so dissimilar effort must be made to reconnect African American culture to its original West African heritage within the landscape of the academic resources available today.

The fact that African Americans are still not offered in the United States today a clear academic link to their original traditional cultural heritage makes it clear that the traditional Western academic elite was not prepared to culturally link the foundation of the music of the most powerful nation on Earth today i.e. the United States, to the culture and benefits of the medieval Empire of Mali, West Africa given that its musical progenitors came as slaves but why? because music is an expression of cultural power.

The ancestry of the music and culture of the Empire of Mali and its cultural and musical vector i.e. the ngoni/banjo has been well documented by

---

74 Agawu, Kofi. *Representing African Music*. London: Routledge, 2003.
75 Hiebert, Paul. *Transformative Worldviews*. MI: Baker Publishing, 1987.

Wesleyan professor Eric Charry in his book entitled "Mande Music" (2000)[76]. In this book, he examines the music, songs, and the instruments of the celebrated and well documented Empire of Mali West Africa, its artistic culture from the 10th – 14th century, and its important legacy enshrined in the academic libraries of its governing cities Timbuktu, Djenne, Gao, Niani and Segou. His book also demonstrates that the anteriority and historicity of well-established standards of aesthetics exist in West African culture hundreds of years before the Slave Trade and that it is just a function of academic logic to deduct that these West African populations will bring the bulk of their musical aesthetics and culture to the Southern plantations of the North American colonies, why? Because the crossing of the Atlantic Ocean referred to as the Middle Passage during the period of the Atlantic Slave Trade was sixty days and nobody forgets his/her culture in sixty days, quite the contrary. Furthermore, evidence of tuning systems of the pentatonic and various heptatonic inclusive of the diatonic systems exist in West Africa in the tonal patterns of the fixed tone balafon (ancestor of the xylophone) that was created to be played in duets with the kora (21 royal string instrument) is described in the instrumentation of the royal courts of the cultural cities of Timbuktu and Djenne, Mali.

To anchor the historical perspectives set out by professor Charry, professor Jacqueline Cogdell Dje Dje from UCLA adds in her 2008 academic works entitled "Fiddling in West Africa"[77] that fiddling and string instruments are as African as its history. Professor Dje Dje describes the history of West Africa's fiddling, the meaning of the performances, and the rituals attached to the ceremonies accompanying these ancestral West African traditions. Dr. Cogdell Dje Dje looks specifically at three ethnic groups in West Africa (Fulbe, Hausas, Dagbamba) who will be part of the contingent of West Africans taken through the second period of the Atlantic Slave Trade led by France, Great Britain, and the Dutch empires. This makes the argument that the ngoni (Malinke term for banjo), its musical sonic aesthetics and the culture of fiddling is as ancient as its West African communities. The author remarks that the Fulbes or Fulanis, Hausas, and Dagbambas are culturally closely related to the Malinke people of the Empire of Mali (10th-14th and the Soninke people of the medieval Empire of Ghana (4th – 10th) from which the Empire of Mali is issued.

We should note that Christian scholar Roberta King in her 2019 book entitled "Global Arts & Christian Witness" remarked that among the Senufos (another Malinke ethnic group of Mali, West Africa) that when listening to the power of the ancestral balafon (ancestor of the xylophone 11th century, Mali, West Africa) being performed by the locals that "this is one of the places where God is making himself known through music", thus describing the spiritual place music plays in its relationship to the concept of the possession of the spirit or Holy ghost through music in ancestral West African societies.

Of all the literature review documents, the book by professors James and Lois Horton entitled "Slavery & the Making of America"[78] published by Oxford University Press in 2005 makes

---

76 Charry, Eric. *Mande Music*. Chicago University Press, 2000.
77 Cogdell Dje Dje, Jacqueline. *Fiddling in West Africa*. Indiana University Press, 2008.
78 James Oliver Horton, Lois E. Horton. *Slavery and the Making of America*. Oxford University Press, 2005.

the clearest connection to the banjo and the culture of the music of West Africa when the authors are referencing President Jefferson at Monticello talking about this most unusual instrument "his slaves are playing and that that he has never seen which he (Jefferson) refers to as the original of the guitar". What this book indicates is that even after the American independence most Whites and even highly educated Whites had never heard of the banjo thus making the point that it was an authentic West African instrument. Furthermore, the Hortons develop the argument that given that West Africans were the first population to introduce the cultivation of rice in the Carolinas, it demonstrated that these enslaved populations came from agrarian communities of West Africa who had demonstrable "well-developed craft traditions and accomplished artists and artisans who worked with wood, metals, yarns, reeds, grasses, and clay. Music, strung and percussion instruments singing, and dancing was integral to these African cultures, as was the storytelling common to oral traditions".

It is an academic fact today that between the 4th and 17th century medieval West Africa was culturally and militarily dominated by three major empires, they were; the Empire of Ghana (no relationship to current Ghana of the Gold Coast) from the 6th-10th, the Empire of Mali 10th-14th and the Empire of Songhai 14th-17th (Davidson, 1998).[79] The Empire of Mali is the better documented medieval cultural institution of West Africa given the size of its trade routes and celebrated exports of salt and gold to Europe and Asia Minor as well as the wealth displayed by

one of its most eulogized leader Emperor Mansa Musa (Al Umari, Levinson, 1981). The argument to document the West African provenance of the banjo and its sonic aesthetics wouldn't be complete unless one would add the work by professor Conway in her 1995 book entitled "African Banjo Echoes in Appalachia: A Study of Folk Traditions"[80] describing the anteriority of both the presence of former African enslaved populations in the Appalachia region but also its musical culture anchored in the music, song repertoire and technical practice of the banjo before the arrival of Europeans in these parts of the United States. Her book also describes how African American banjo players taught their instruments to these European populations of Celtic origins before and while the Civil War raged on. The transfer of these African aesthetics will shape the expression of Celtic culture in a unique way to create the indigenous and authentic Bluegrass music of the Appalachian regions. One of the puzzling issues that make the role of the banjo as a fundamentally important part of African culture in America has to do with the reality that African Americans will cease to play their instrument when it becomes the musical instrument of choice of White actors and dancers during the minstrelsy period of the 19th and early 20th century American entertainment. White entertainment establishment appropriation of this instrument so central to the identity of Africans in America coupled with the systematic dehumanization of Blacks in America and the national effort to caricature them in demeaning ways throughout the world via the "Black Face minstrelsy" provoked inside the Black communities a

79 Davidson, Basil. *Africa Series*. Davidson Collection, 1984.
80 Conway, Cecelia. *African Banjo Echoes in Appalachia: A Study of Folk Traditions* . Knoxville, TN: University of Tennessee Press, 1995.

knee jerk effect that lead Africans in America to reject their ancestral African instrument as early as the 1920s in America.

Professor Laurent Dubois, author of the 2016 book entitled "The Banjo: America's African Instrument"[81] published by Harvard University makes the compelling argument that the banjo was the instrument that from the 1600s forward allowed Africans in bondage in the Caribbean and North America to maintain and retain their musical traditions through the oral tradition and the use of their ancestral African string instruments carved out of gourds and covered with skins before it became industrialized as the essential musical instrument of White expression of Black minstrelsy The book demonstrates that the demeaning socio-cultural effect of the minstrelsy played a significant role in the African communities of the Americas in their decision to move away from the banjo.

In all fairness, and given the mounting amount of academic information that exists it is most curious that academia has not come out forcefully to claim that American popular music's foundation comes from the West African aesthetics of the sonic expression of the Western musicologists' own recognition of "blue notes" (Allen, 1859)[82] and that this African musical tapestry of "blue notes" had existed hundreds of years before the Atlantic Slave trade through the well-documented craftsmanship of string instruments in evidence in the medieval Empires of Ghana, Mali, and Songhai and that these sonic expressions in tandem with the banjo provided the necessary cultural framework for the creation of the well-established Blues tonalities here in North America. The academic absence of definitive recognition of West African culture and influence in American music at the ethnomusicology level is even more startling because definitive academic information regarding the role that music plays in ethnic identity formation in the diaspora has been recognized in many academic disciplines whether in social sciences, such as sociology, psychology, psychiatry, etc...

Rolf Lidskog's[83] article precisely entitled "The Role of Music in Ethnic Identity Formation in the Diaspora: A Research Review" published in 2017, describes in-depth the socio-cultural elements that define the role of music in the context of ethnic identity formation specifically as it applies to the diaspora. Culture is described here as a process defined by cultural resources, artifacts, rituals, knowledge, and sonic expressions that provide the basis for a continuum although unstable of the construction and the cultural renegotiations of ethnic identities worldwide. These general concepts are helpful analytical tools as they offer a macro picture of the socio-cultural elements present in the psychology of migrating populations in defining what is important for their identities concerning their sonic expression or music.

Furthermore, author and Harvard professor Eileen Southern in her book entitled "The Music of Black Americans: A History" published by Norton in 1997 describes at length and in detail the melodic contours, harmonic colors, and rhythmic patterns brought by West Africans in bondage to the Southern plantations of the

81 Dubois, Laurent. *The Banjo: America's African Instrument.* Harvard Publisher, 2016.

82 Allen, Willian Francis. *Slave Songs of the United States.* Dover, 1867/1995.

83 Lidskog, Rolf. *The Role of Music in Ethnic Identity Formation in the Diaspora: A Research Review.* Authors International Social Science Journal, Wiley Publisher, 2017.

South. She details the practice of the banjo but even includes a reference to the "balaphone" in the Louisiana Gazette of 1810. This is significant because the term "balaphone" is the Malinke term given to the African ancestor of the marimba or xylophone of the populations of Mali. In Malinke, the term "Balafon" comes from the sentence "Bala na Fo" which means "to make the wood speak". The fact that this instrument traveled to Louisiana in and around the beginning of the 19th century demonstrates that people from that region and these musical aesthetics were part of a continuum of enslaved people from West Africa who were still coming to our shores with their musical culture.

As a demonstration of cross-cultural fertilization thus, implying separate cultural influences coming together scholar Robert Winans[84] in his 2018 book entitled "Banjo, Roots and Branches" tells the story of the banjo's journey from Africa to the western hemisphere. In it, he blends the music, history, and describes a union of cultures culminating into America's authentic musical form called Bluegrass. The book covers West African origins, the adaptations, and the movement of the instrument in the Caribbean and United States. There is additional detailed ethnographic and technical information on gourds, lutes of West African origin, which supports the argument that the banjo was a key vector of cultural African retention.

Thus the question becomes if Western academia can recognize that Bluegrass music is an authentically indigenous American music fused from European Celtic roots, why can't it recognize that the sonic, rhythmic, and melodic tapestry of the Blues that animates Bluegrass is from the culture of the dominant Empires of West Africa and in particular that of the medieval Empire of Mali since it has been recorded and widely documented in history as a prestigious cultural powerhouse who established the ngoni (ancestor of the banjo) and the balafon (fixed tone ancestor of the xylophone) and whose cultural influence ranged from as far West of Senegal, Gambia and Guinea and as far east in West Africa to the delta of Nigeria named after its river Niger? While the question remains, the academic weight of the literature review compels us to affirmatively conclude that there is ample evidence that the foundation of African American music in North America comes from the culture of West Africa dominated by the three medieval empires of Ghana, Mali, and Songhai that established some of the African instruments that have been cataloged and have defined the musical repertoire of Nashville, Tennessee i.e. the banjo, the musical culture of the Mississippi Delta through the Blues and the aesthetic revolution of the African American Gospel phenomenon that the white American clergy will re-baptize as Negro-Spirituals from which America's defining art form Jazz will emerge to lift this nation to the status of a cultural superpower thanks to the unfettered genius of King Oliver, Louis Armstrong, Duke Ellington, Art Tatum, Charlie Parker, Dizzy Gillespie, Miles Davis, John Coltrane and more.

---

84   Winans, Robert. *Banjo, Roots and Branches*. University of Illinois Press, 2018.

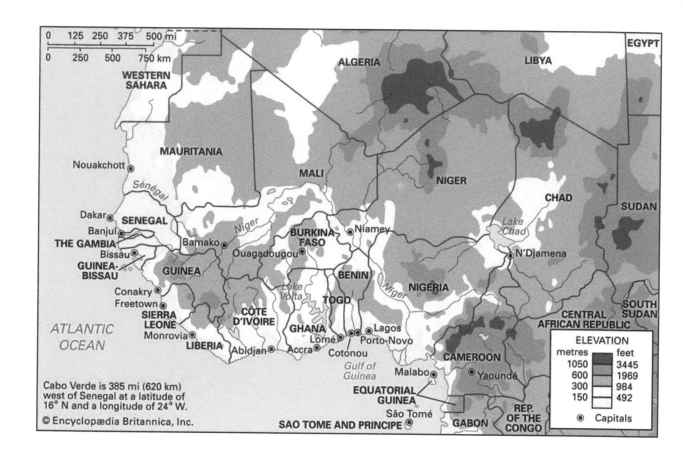

0 125 250 375 500 mi
0 250 500 750 km

EGYPT

WESTERN
SAHARA

ALGERIA

LIBYA

MAURITANIA

Nouakchott

Sénégal

MALI

NIGER

CHAD

SUDAN

Dakar
Banjul
SENEGAL
THE GAMBIA
Bissau
GUINEA-
BISSAU

Bamako

Niger

BURKINA
FASO

Níamey

Lake
Chad

N'Djamena

Ouagadougou

GUINEA

Conakry
Freetown
SIERRA
LEONE
Monrovia
LIBERIA

CÔTE
D'IVOIRE

*Lake
Volta*

BENIN

TOGO

GHANA

Abidjan

Accra

Lomé

Niger

NIGERIA

Lagos
Porto-Novo
Cotonou

SOUTH
SUDAN

CENTRAL
AFRICAN REPUBLIC

ATLANTIC
OCEAN

Cabo Verde is 385 mi (620 km)
west of Senegal at a latitude of
16° N and a longitude of 24° W.

© Encyclopædia Britannica, Inc.

*Gulf of
Guinea*

Malabo

CAMEROON

Yaoundé

EQUATORIAL
GUINEA

São Tomé

SAO TOME AND PRINCIPE

GABON

REP.
OF THE
CONGO

ELEVATION
metres   feet
1050   3445
600   1969
300   984
150   492

⊙   Capitals

Chapter 5

West Africa; Mali, Senegal, Guinea, Nigeria, Ghana, Mauritania

Mali

Mali, officially known as the republic of Mali is the eight-largest country in Africa and 25th largest country in the world. Mali is a landlocked and covers a total area of 1,240,192 square kilometers. The total land surface sums around 1,220,190sq kilometers whereas, the rest of the 20,002sq. kilometers is the water surface from the third largest river in Africa, the Niger River. Its capital is Bamako. Mali is named after one of the wealthiest and famous West African empires that of Mali. It ruled over the region between the 10th and the 17th centuries evolving from the 6th century Empire of Ghana, to the 10th century Empire of Mali to the 14th century Empire of Songhai. At its peak the Empire of Mali and its military controlled the totality of the trade routes from the Atlantic Coast to the Arabic Peninsula through Egypt. Home to a massive population of 20,137,527people, 60% of Mali's population is under the age of 25 as per the survey conducted in 2017. The 19th century marks the scramble of Africa when France seized control of Mali, making it a part of French Sudan which later joined hands with Senegal in 1956.

However, the collision of the French Sudan and Senegal resulted in the Mali federation in 1960 which was later declared as the republic of Mali by the Sudanese republic after the withdrawal of Senegal.

Mali generates most of its revenue thanks to gold mining and extensive agricultural exports. In fact, almost 80% of the export earnings are from cotton and gold exports. However, due to fluctuations in gold prices as well as the amount of agricultural harvest and commodity generated, Mali's fiscal status is always shifting.

More than half of Mali's land area is categorized as desert or considerably 'semi-desert' due to the riverine area irrigated by the Niger River. Taking up to 65% of the landmass of Mali, it is also the biggest reason for the country's economic activity. Almost 10% of Mali's population is nomadic, whereas the majority, 80%, is acquitted in the labor workforce taken up for farming and fishing. Most industrial activity can be credited to processing work for farming commodities. Moreover, the government authorities finance the production of cereals. It decreases Mali's dependency on imported food items and susceptibility to experiencing unprecedented price shocks.

Ethnic Groups

Incorporating various ethnic groups under a single flag, Following are mostly commonly found within the vicinity of the republic of Mali.

- Bambara 33.3%,
- Fulani (Peuhl) 13.3%,
- Sarakole/Soninke/Marka 9.8%,
- Senufo/Manianka 9.6%,
- Malinke 8.8%,
- Dogon 8.7%,
- Sonrai 5.9%,
- Bobo 2.1%,
- Tuareg/Bella 1.7%,
- Other Malian 6%, from members of Economic Community of West Africa .4%, other .3% (2018 est.)

Language

There are 13 national languages of Mali in addition to its unofficial language as stated below;

- French (official),
- Bambara 46.3%, Peuhl/Foulbe 9.4%,
- Dogon 7.2%, Maraka/Soninke 6.4%,
- Malinke 5.6%, Sonrhai/Djerma 5.6%.

The president serves as a chief of state and commander in chief of the armed forces. A prime minister appointed by the president serves as head of government and in turn appoints the Council of Ministers.

Contemporary Music

Cheick Tidiane Seck

Cheick Tidiane Seck was born on 11th December 1953. He is a Malian composer, arranger, and keyboard player. He is an artist of enormous musical stature who has worked in varied musical settings ranging from the Rock and Blues idioms with Carlos Santana to Jazz styling with Joe Zawinul. He is also a music producer in great demand. Having been a headliner at Jazz and music festivals worldwide for the last four decades, he is steeped in the musical traditions of his vast Malian heritage. He has led the way as a composer and instrumentalist in shaping musical compositions that are deeply rooted in his West African culture but have showcased a remarkable openness

and subtle integration of musical cultural concepts beyond borders. A virtuoso keyboardist, experts consider him one of the most influential composers of note hailing from the continent of Africa today.

Ali Farka Toure

Ali Farka Touré was born in 1939 in the village of Kanau, on the banks of the Niger River in Gourma-Rharous Cercle in the northwestern Malian region of Tombouctou. He was a Malian singer and multi-instrumentalist, and one of the African continent's most internationally renowned musicians. His music blends traditional Malian music and its derivatives. He sang in several African languages, ranging from Songhay, Fulea, to Tamasheq or Bambara as on his breakthrough album, Ali Farka Touré, which established his reputation in the world music community.

Ali Farka Toure is the light that shone on the cultural and musical connections that existed between West African musical traditions and culture and the music of African Americans in the Southern plantations brought over during the period of the Atlantic Slave Trade starting in the 16th century. The virtuoso guitarist and vocalist Ali Farka Toure said "In anthropology the term Black American... that does not exist...but they are Blacks in America...which means that ...they came with their culture...". This seemingly benign statement of the obvious by this master musician turned out to be revolutionary for it lit a fire in academia that led to many scholarly publications depicting the importance of West African music and culture as foundational vectors of cultural identities that would shape the music of the United States forever through the Blues of the Mississippi Delta. Ethnomusicologist and Blues and Country music master guitarist Ry Cooder is credited for making that cultural connection with Ali Farka Toure's Songhai music early on. Ali Farka Toure passed March 6, 2006.

Salif Keita

Salif Keita was born on 25th august 1949 as a traditional prince in the village of Djoliba. His music combines traditional West African musical styles. He is a Malian singer-songwriter known for blending elements of a wide range of local African—especially Mande—music traditions with jazz, rhythm and blues, and other international popular-music styles to pioneer the Afropop dance-music

genre. His highly successful debut album, Soro (1987), was a remarkable multicultural achievement. Hailed as "The Voice of Africa" he is one of the most powerful and influential vocalists in the world. He has single handedly transformed contemporary West African music vocally, texturally but also melodically and harmonically. A heavenly gifted vocalist, he has combined the power of vocal emotions with positive messaging throughout his career. Anchored in the musical Malinke traditions of his royal lineage but always open to musical experimentations he has been referred to as a trailblazer for music and social causes worldwide. His personal socio-cultural travails with albinism in Africa have made him one of the most effective spokesperson to address such social ills.

Traditional Music

Around the 10th century AD, the Empire of Mali took over and gradually expanded the real estate of the 6th century Empire of Ghana of the Soninke people located in parts of current Senegal (no relationship to current country of Ghana). The Empire of Mali developed a music anchored in the culture and aesthetics of the people of the Mande region of West Africa. A rich cultural history musically and melodically enshrined in the accomplishments and the epic narratives of its first emperor, the famed Soundiata Keita still celebrated today. A musical guild supported by the royal courts was established. That guild is called "Djalis" in Malinke which means blood as a symbol of the importance of the dispensation of the historical cultural continuum of the Mande community. The metaphor is telling. The Djalis are the historical, cultural and artistic repository of the culture and history of the people of the Mande of Mali. The Djalis or (griots in English) are acknowledged by the last names they carry such as Kouyate, Diabate, Cissokho, Susso and other national related versions of these last names throughout West Africa.

Toumani Diabate

Born on August 10, 1965, Toumani Diabaté is a Malian master kora player. He comes from a long family tradition of kora players, including his father Sidiki Diabaté, who recorded the first ever kora album in 1970. The Diabate family belongs to the guild of the musicians of the Royal courts of the medieval Empires of Mali and Songhai called Djalis. The Diabates are master kora players and holders of the history and cultural heritage of the Mande traditions. Toumani Diabate is the 70th torch holder of the Mande cultural and musical traditions of the Diabate clan of Mali. He is a Kora master of dazzling speed and unparalleled technique. He has single handedly expanded worldwide the reach and the horizon of the royal West African harp with 21 strings we call Kora along with its musical repertoire.

His collaborations with musicians all over the world have garnered rave reviews and he continues to be a sought after mentor and teacher. It is worth noting that the Malinke term Kora "means singing in Greek" and that the term for music in Arabic before Islam is "Djaliyah" from the Malinke term "Djalis" which gives credence to the incredible ancestry of that culture of West Africa and its ancestral musical influence and reach worldwide. In addition to performing the traditional music of Mali, he has also been involved in cross-cultural collaborations with flamenco (born out of the Malian culture of music brought by the Moors), blues, jazz, and other international styles.

Bazoumana Cissoko

Born blind in 1890 in Segou, Banzumana is considered to be the Dean of the Malian musical tradition. He interpreted an immensely rich repertoire of traditional music and songs of the empires of Mali and Songhai. He is also credited with composing a great number of songs which are noteworthy for none of them contained praises for a living person. He was a master instrumentalist of the Ngoni (ancestor of the banjo) whose legend has it that it was dotted of supernatural powers for his instrument was able to fly and play while he slept. One of Banzumana's compositions became the national anthem of Mali with lyrics written by the eminent Malian literary scholar Dr. Seydou Badian Kouyate.

Bassekou Kouyate

Born in 1966 in Garana, Barouéli Cercle, a few kilometers from Ségou, Bassekou Kouyaté is a musician from Mali. He is considered a master of an instrument called "the ngoni" and ancestor of the North American banjo brought over during the period of the Atlantic Slave Trade. The ngoni is an ancient traditional lute originating and popularized in West Africa. His band is known as Ngoni Ba. Kouyaté's debut album, Segu Blue, was released internationally in 2007 by Outhere Records and distributed in the U.K. by Proper Music Distribution. Bassekou was a true artist, and that showed in his collaborative efforts. Over time he had many popular musicians on his collaboration list from both in and outside of Mali. From the works of Youssou N'Dour to Ali Farka Toure, The Kronos Quartet, Bela Fleck, Taj Mahal, and Eliades Ochoa, to name a few – he had worked with all.

Moreover, he was an essential musician as part of Ali Farka Toure's posthumous album 'Savane,' released in July 2006. To add more to his coveted achievements as a musician, Baasekou was part of Taj Mahal's 'Kulanjan' project and played in the Symmetric trio alongside Toumani Diabate (kora). As a performer, Bassekou has demonstrated to the world that the Malian Ngoni is the ancestor of the American banjo and that this West African instrument served as the cultural vector of African aesthetics so important to the identity markers of these West African populations brought to the Southern plantations of the nascent United States through the Atlantic Slave Trade. These West African populations will single-handedly re-create an African-based culture in North America through the inflections of the West African blue notes. Hence the Blues, rhythmic syncopations, call and response systems, and a ternary appreciation and subdivision of time generated a sense of pulse that was termed "Swing" by America's most celebrated composer, Jazz Great Duke Ellington.

Guinea

Guinea officially the Republic of Guinea is a coastal country in West Africa. Formerly known as French Guinea. Stretching to a total area of 245,857 sq km, the land surface is of 245,717 sq km and the Water surface measures 140 sq km. Conakry is the capital of Guinea and it has been named after the Guinea region of West Africa that lies along the Gulf of Guinea and stretches north to the Sahel. Its people belong to twenty-four ethnic groups. The economy is largely dependent on agriculture and mineral production. It is the world's second largest producer of bauxite, and has rich deposits of diamonds and gold. Furthermore, the country is also rich in iron ore, uranium, hydropower, fish, and salt.

The population in the country is estimated to be around 12,877,894. It is a predominantly Islamic country, with Muslims representing 85 percent of the population. Guinea's strong population growth is a result of declining mortality rates and sustained elevated fertility. The population growth rate was somewhat tempered in the 2000s because of a period of net outmigration.

Ethnic groups

Demographics of racial and religious affiliations of people living in Guinea represents the practice of 24 ethnic groups within the country. However, out of them following are the dominating ones with the given ratio;

- ◆ Fulani (Peuhl) 33.4%,
- ◆ Malinke 29.4%,
- ◆ Susu 21.2%,
- ◆ Guerze 7.8%,
- ◆ Kissi 6.2%,
- ◆ Toma 1.6%,
- ◆ Other/foreign .4% (2018 est.)

With different ethnic groups growing under the same flag, 89.1% of the population is Muslim, 6.8% Christians, 26.6% animist.

Language

With French being the official language spoken in schools, offices, and government administration, there are more than 40 languages spoken alone in Guinea. However, Pular, Maninka, Susu, and a few other native languages are most common to be heard.

Political Affiliation

It is a democratic republic with a president, a prime minister and a representative national assembly.

Contemporary Music

The historical, cultural and musical perspective of today's country of Guinea is entirely connected to the history, cultures and music of the three massive medieval empires of West Africa namely, Ghana, Mali and Songhai. West Africa is unified culturally while still remaining diverse in its regional appreciation of that central conceptual culture. The original balafon (ancestor of the xylophone) is still in state in the village of Niagassola, Guinea. This instrument central to the culture and music of the medieval empires of West Africa for its imposition of the concept of fixed tonalities' aesthetics is a testimony to the cultural contributions and the importance of the Guinean populations in connection to the culture of West Africa as a whole. The military and cultural accomplishments of the legendary King of the Susus, Soumanguru Kante are an intrinsic and essential part of the epic narratives of the royal mythology of the medieval empires of West Africa linking the Empire of Ghana, Mali and Songhai.

Mory Kante

Mory Kanté was a Guinean vocalist and player of the kora harp. He was born in Albadaria, French Guinea on 29th march 1950. He was a singer, songwriter, multi-instrumentalist, and one of West Africa's most versatile and commercially successful musical pioneers. He was best known internationally for his 1987 hit song "Yé ké yé ké", which reached number- one in Belgium, Finland, the Netherlands, and Spain. The album it came from, Akwaba Beach, was the best-selling African record of its time. He passed away May 22, 2020 in Conakry at the age of 70.

Mamadou Diabate

Mamadou Diabaté was born in Kita, Mali in 1975 in a griot family. Mamadou Diabaté is a Malian musician known for his work with the kora. He is a descendant of a griot family that has played music since the 13th century with notable family members including Toumani Diabaté. He has released numerous albums including his debut album, Tunga, and the Grammy nominated album Behmanka.

Sekou Diabate

Born on July 8, 1944, in Tiro (Faranah region), Sékou Diabaté is a Guinean guitarist and co-founder of the band Bembeya Jazz in 1961. He has been the director of Bembeya Jazz since 2003. Even though his full name is Sékouba Diabaté, he is mostly referred to as Sékou Bembeya Diabaté. As there is a namesake of Diabaté is already present nicknamed Sékouba Bambino. So for specification in reference, people have nicknamed him "Diamond fingers." A virtuoso guitarist, he has transferred the melodic, harmonic, and rhythmic concepts of the Kora and the Ngoni to the guitar with unparalleled skills. His improvisation flights have delighted music aficionados worldwide. He is the pride of his nation and recognized from coast to coast as one of the most important guitarists on the continent of Africa.

Traditional Music

Fodéba Keïta

Born on 19th January 1921 in Siguiri, Fodéba Keïta was a Guinean dancer, musician, writer, playwright, composer and politician. He was the founder of the first professional African theatrical troupe, Theatre Africain. He also arranged Liberté, the national anthem of Guinea. He began his artistic career while he was pursuing a law degree in Paris in 1948. He founded the band Sud Jazz. Beginning in the late 1940s, he founded founded the most important Théâtre Africain which later became the national dance company of Guinea. He was one of the most ardent cultural architects of the resurgence of West African music and dance worldwide and a great proponent of Panafricanism through the dissemination of culture. West Africa never had a greater cultural ambassador than in the person of Fodeba Keita. He passed away May 27, 1969 at Camp Boiro.

El Hadj Djeli Sory Kouyate

Consistent with the cultural and musical importance of the three medieval empires of West Africa namely Ghana, Mali and Songhai, the 1918 born Guinean El Hadj Djeli Sory Kouyate is considered as one of the world's most renowned balafon players. Descended from Bala Fasseke Kouyate, djeli (first court musician) in the court of Sundiata Keita, the 11th century founder of the Empire of Mali, Sory Kouyate hails from a very influential musical family. Two of his brothers served as Djalis in the court of King Nalotaye in Kantande. Generations

GUINÉE : ANTHOLOGIE DU BALAFON MANDINGUE
Guinea : An anthology of the Mandingo balaphone

of some of the best musicians to ever be born in the African nation have been attributed to El Hadj thanks to his prestigious Ensemble Instrumental National of Guinea where he served as the director. He made his debut album at the age of 73 named as Anthologie du Balafon Mandigue, Vol. 1. His musical association with Fodeba Keita was legendary and his instrumental work with vocalist Sory Kandia Kouyate remains memorable for the ages.

Mauritania

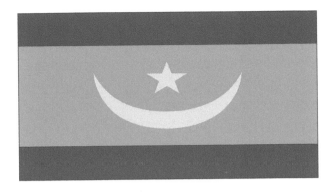

Mauritania officially known as the Islamic Republic of Mauritania is a country in Northwest Africa. It is the twenty-eighth largest country in the world, the eleventh largest sovereign state in Africa, and the largest country lying entirely below an altitude of 1,000 meters (3,300 ft). Mauritania is bordered by the Atlantic Ocean to the west, Western Sahara to the north and northwest, Algeria to the northeast, Mali to the east and southeast, and Senegal to the southwest. The country's name derives from the name of these Black populations from Northern Mali who inhabited that part of West Africa all the way to Morocco called the Moors from which the Berbers will form. Formerly a French colony, Mauritania became an independent state in 1960.

Located on the Atlantic coast, Nouakchott is the capital of the country and also the largest city. Stretching to 1,030,700 sq km, the total surface area is in Sahara. The total population in the region is around 4 million. With a sustained total fertility rate of about 4 children per woman and almost 60% of the population under the age of 25, Mauritania's population is likely to continue growing for the foreseeable future.

Mauritania's economy is dominated by extractive industries (oil and mines), fisheries, livestock, agriculture, and services. Half the population still

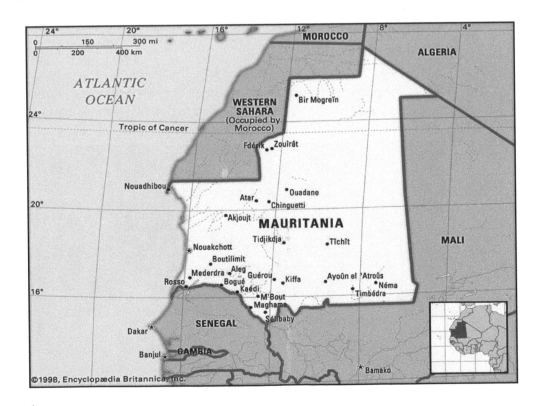

depends on farming and raising livestock, even though many nomads and subsistence farmers were forced into the cities by recurrent droughts in the 1970s, 1980s, 2000s, and 2017. Recently, GDP growth has been driven largely by foreign investment in the mining and oil sectors. Mauritania's extensive mineral resources include iron ore, gold, copper, gypsum, and phosphate rock, and exploration is ongoing for tantalum, uranium, crude oil, and natural gas.

Ethnic Groups

The largest group is the Haratin, or so-called "Black Moors". The Haratin make up 40% of the population One of the other ethnic groups is the Bidhan. The Bidhan represent approximately a quarter of the population. The rest of the inhabitants belong to sub-Saharan ethnic groups. These sub- Saharan ethnic groups are non-Arabic speaking and are largely resident in or originating from the Senegal River Valley, including Halpulaar, Fulani, Soninke, Wolof, and Bambara ethnic groups. The population is mostly Sunni Muslims.

Language

The official language of Mauritania is Arabic. However, the Arabic spoken in this region is quite different from the modern standard Arabic as it includes a lot of Berber words. Bearing a history as the colony of France, French is also widely spoken in the region along with other national languages, Pular, Soninke, and Wolof.

Political Affiliation

It is an Islamic republic with a president who holds executive powers and with elected officials to the representative Assembly.

Contemporary Music

Tinariwen

Unlike other acclaimed individual artists, Tinariwen is a group formed by singers, songwriters, and musicians from the Sahara Desert region of Mali. Founded in Tamanrassat, Algeria, by Ibrahim Ag Alhabib in 1979, the Tuareg musicians

returned to Mali after a peace agreement was signed between 1990 and 1995 by the various factions of the Rebellion and the Malian government.

The very first traction that Tinariwen gained outside the Saharan region was in 2001 when the release of their album The Radio Tisdas Sessions made waves. Soon they were seen performing at the Festival au Désert in Mali and the Roskilde Festival in Denmark.

In 2007, the release of the album Aman Iman marked a turning point, and NPR called the group "music's true rebels." The Tinariwen sonic landscape is primarily guitar-driven, known as assouf among the Tuareg people. The typical styles have their origin in West Africa and a few other music forms/styles practiced by Berber and Tuareg Berber.

Tinariwen takes their inspiration for creating music from Malian musicians. The group currently has 6 active members—Ibrahim Ag Alhabib, Alhassane Ag Touhami, Abdallah Ag Alhousseyni, Eyadou Ag Leche, Said Ag Ayad, and Elaga Ag Hamid. They sing about the Tuareg rebellion and the socio-economic difficulties the Tuareg people faced with the coming to an end of their ancestral nomadic lifestyle due to European colonization and border partitioning of Africa resulting from the Bismarck conference 1884.

Women's Group Tartit

Tartit is a group composed of five women originally from Timbuktu, Mali who found refuge in a camp in Mauretania in 1992. Led by Fadimata Walett Oumar they sing in Tamasheq one of the Tuaregs languages. They incorporated electric instruments to their cultural traditional renditions to great acclaim. They toured Europe ad the Unites States in 1998 and 2000. They have been active at

the United Nations level in raising awareness for the culture and heritage of the Tuareg people of Northern Mali. Their association goes beyond musical performances and includes generating opportunities for the creation of schools for children and economic opportunities for women in that part of the world. They are immensely active in the area of women's rights and political engagement.

Senegal

Senegal is officially known as the Republic of Senegal. It is a country in West Africa bordered by Mauritania in the north, Mali to the east, Guinea to the southeast, and Guinea-Bissau to the southwest. Senegal's economic and political capital is Dakar. This regional area was part of the glorious era of the three major empires of West Africa. It was part of the Empire of Ghana, Mali and Songhai from the 6th until the 17th century. Later on this regional area of West Africa was also known for his kingdoms of Cayor, Baol, Serer and Djola. In the 19th century, it became part of French Sudan and a colony of France. Military battles against the French military led by the royal descendent of the Woloff Kingdom Lat Dior Latir Diop resulted in this part of West Africa gaining its independence from the French under the term of Federation of Mali in 1958. The federation was

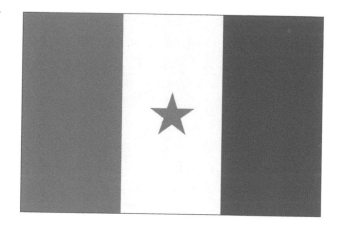

to have two leaders; Modibo Keita and Leopold Sedar Senghor. The political cohabitation did not last long and the country of Senegal was created in 1960 as a result of the political split. Senegal's territory included the land area controlled by the Soninkes, the Wolofs, the Toucouleurs, the Pulaars, the Serers, the Diolas, the Mandjak and the Mankagn and extended

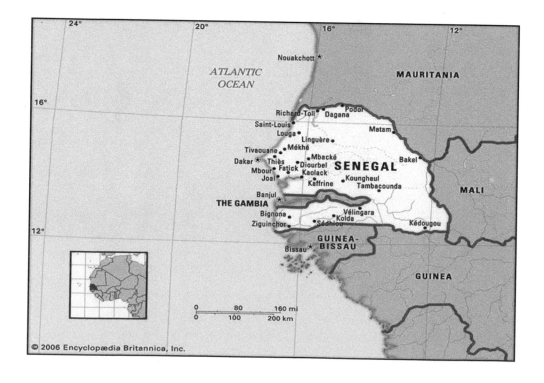

© 2006 Encyclopædia Britannica, Inc.

from the regional area west of the river that carried its name to the Atlantic Ocean.

The country owes its name to the Senegal River, which borders it to the east and north. Senegal covers a land area of almost 196,722 square kilometers out of which 192,530 sq km is land and 4,192 sq km water. It has a population of around 15.7 million.

Its economy is essentially based on agriculture. Senegal has suffered in the last decades of extensive droughts and the desertification process induced by climate change has had dire consequences on its economy.

Ethnic Groups

Home to several ethnic groups, the country has following ethnic groups in majority. Wolof 37.1%,, Pular 26.2%, Serer 17%, Mandinka 5.6%, Jola 4.5%, Soninke 1.4%, other 8.3% (includes Europeans and persons of Lebanese descent) (2017 est.) Senegal is mostly a muslin country with 95.9% Muslims and only 4.1% Christians living within the vicinity.

Language

With French being the official language of the country, there are also other languages spoken around the country including Wolof, Pular, Jola, Mandinka, Serer, and Soninke.

Political Affiliations

Senegal is a democratic republic. The president is both the head of the government and the chief of the state. It has a representative legislative assembly.

Contemporary Music

Youssou Ndour

Youssou N'Dour was born on 1st October 1959. Being the pioneer of mbalax—a Senegalese popular music style that blends Wolof traditional instrumental rhythms and vocal forms inclusive of Cuban and other Latin American popular genres. He is a Senegalese singer, songwriter, composer, actor, businessman and politician. He is a gifted of an extraordinary vocal range. He began his career as early as the age of 12 years old. He is the first Senegalese international superstar in contemporary terms and he has been in films such as Return to Gorée (2007), Youssou N'Dour: I Bring What I Love (2008), You Africa and

Amazing Grace. He is hailed as one of the most important musicians of Africa today. His band included the infinitely talented percussionist Mbaye Dieye Faye and the renowned bassist Habib Faye. A UNICEF goodwill ambassador, Youssou Ndour's contributions to the development of African music worldwide are enormous and his talent has made him one of the most recognizable voices on the continent of Africa and abroad.

Ismaël Lô

Ismaël Lô was born on 30th August 1956 in Dogondoutchi, Niger. He is a Senegalese musician, songwriter, singer, and an actor. He is also known for playing guitar and harmonica, and has been called "the Bob Dylan of Africa". In the 1970s, he studied at the School of Art in Dakar. He later joined the popular group Super Diamono, but left in 1984 to start a solo career. Over the next four years Lo recorded five popular solo albums. He also been a part of Ousmane Sembene's Camp de Thiaroye. He later recorded a couple of albums with soft guitar melodies and traditional Senegalese mbalax. He is a celebrated artist in Senegal and his national reach has begun to expand worldwide.

Xalam II

Xalam is a Senegalese musical group founded in 1969. It was founded by a group of friends interested in playing Rock, Bossa, Salsa, Rhythms and Blues. The band was originally called African Khalam Orchestra. The band was actually named after the instrument Xalam. Xalam performed a mix of contemporary jazz tunes as well as African originals. The band in-

cluded sax, drums, African percussion, bass, and electric guitar. It recorded a couple of albums over the period of years including Daïda (1975), Ade (1979), Gorée (1983), Africa (1984), Live à Montreux (2008), and Waxati (2015). The band Xalam contributed great energy to the development of Afrobeat music in Senegal as its members kept an ear to the contemporary sounds of

African bands such as Osibisa, Fela Kuti, Manu Dibango, Ifanbondi etc…and as a result they were able to fashion a new dynamic style of African music that blended soulfully and successfully many genres of African and African American music. Its leader, the powerhouse drummer Prosper Niang was the catalyst behind the success of the band and its eminently talented keyboardist Henri Guillabert continues to be the glue that keeps Xalam II together after the passing of its beloved leader in 1988.

Baba Maal

Born in 1953 on the North Eastern region of Senegal in the town of Podor, Baba Maal is one of the great vocalists, guitarists and composers of West Africa. Dotted of an amazing multi octave vocal range and the unique textural and musical culture of its ethnic Pulaar roots he has become one of the great ambassadors of West African culture worldwide. His musical associations with Jazz guitarist Ernest Ranglin and pianist Hank Jones have been heralded as great musical cultural reconnections of the African diaspora.

The quality of his tenor and the texture of his vocals make him the incomparable ambassador of the musical traditions of the populations of the eastern part of Senegal. Discovered and promoted by Island producer Chris Blackwell, Baaba Maal establishes a name for himself worldwide and his collaborations with renowned artists such as Brian Eno, Taj Mahal, and Ernest Ranglin to name a few received rave reviews. Generous and socially conscious Baaba Maal lends his name and support to many social causes including children charities. His 1998 live recording at the Royal Festival Hall is a landmark record and serves as a most important documentary of the aesthetics and musical traditions of the Pular people of Senegal. Baba Maal is a celebrated headliner at major music festivals worldwide and he currently serves also as a United Nations Youth Ambassador.

Traditional Music
Doudou Ndiaye Comba Rose

Doudou Ndiaye Coumba Rose was born on July 28th, 1930 in Dakar, Senegal, into a family of Wolof royals. He was a Senegalese drummer, composer, and band leader of the 20th century. He is the pioneer and the Dean of Senegalese

*Doudou Ndiaye
Comba Rose*

traditional music. He was recognized as the Master of Senegal's traditional drum, the sabar. With his expertise in Sabar, he expanded his vision to include other drums and rhythms such as the saourouba, assicot, bougarabou, meung meung, lambe, n'der, gorom babass, and khine.

The leader of an eponymous 35 to 40 member drum corps, Doudou Ndiaye Rose put the country of Senegal on the world map. While he was alive his mastery of the Sabar drum had no equals. His constant attention to social inequities led him to create an all-female drum ensemble that was unrivaled rhythmically anywhere in the world bucking the common belief that only men master drumming in Africa. His female ensemble "The Rosettes" became a drumming sensation. His mastery and legacy will remain in the hearts and minds of his fans forever as the marvelous documentary entitled " Djabote" filmed on the island of Goree showcased the master drummer leading his majestic family affair, an ensemble of some 40 drummers, with incredible precision and flawless artistry.

In 2006, he was declared a "living human treasure" by the United Nations cultural agency for keeping alive traditional Senegalese rhythms. He is well known around the globe for his recorded drum tracks. He passed away on August 19, 2015.

Foday Musa Suso

Foday Musa Suso was born in Sarre Hamadi Village, Wuli District. He is a Gambian kora musician and composer. Foday was sent to master kora teacher, Sekou Suso in the village of Pasamasi, Wuli District where he was trained until the age of 18. He is known worldwide for his hypnotic performances of traditional Kora (Harp/Lute) music, and his cutting-edge musical encounter and collaborations. He spent many years in Chicago, Illinois, and his musical collaborations have been praised worldwide. They included work with Philip Glass, Pharoah Saunders, Jack De Johnette, Herbie Hancock, Paul Simon, and Ginger Baker among others. Foday Musa Suso contributed music to the 1984 Los Angeles Olympic Games and again in 2004.

Nigeria

Nigeria, officially known as the Federal Republic of Nigeria, is a country in West Africa. Nigeria is a federal republic comprising 36 states and the Federal Capital Territory, where the capital, Abuja, is located. The country was named for the Niger River that flows through the west of the country to the Atlantic Ocean; and the contraction of the two words Niger – and Area by British colonizers. Nigeria borders the country of Niger in the north, Chad in the northeast, Cameroon in

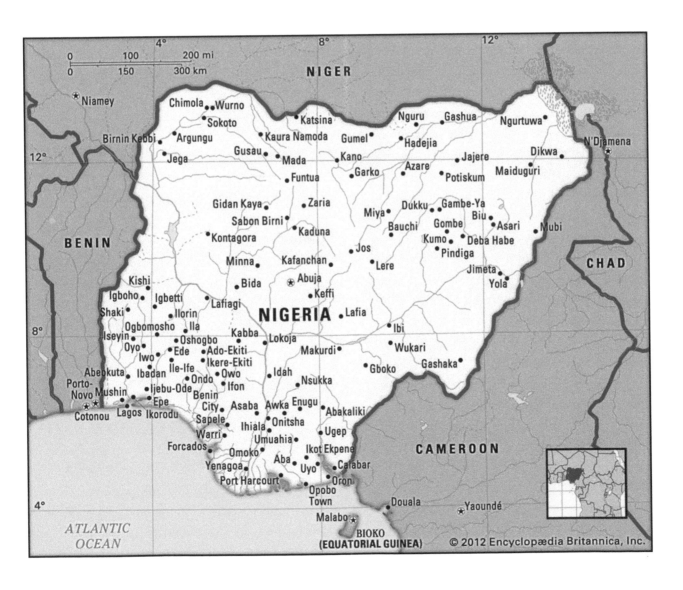

the east, and Benin in the west. Its southern coast is on the Gulf of Guinea in the Atlantic Ocean. Lagos, one of the largest metropolitan areas in the world, is the largest city in Nigeria and the continent of Africa.

Nigeria covers a total area of 923,768 sq km in which 910,768 sq km is land and 13,000 sq km is water. Nigeria is the most populous country in Africa and the seventh-most populous country in the world, with an estimated population of 213 million. Its economy is the largest in Africa, the 26th-largest in the world by nominal GDP, and 25th-largest by PPP. Nigeria has its own currency. This regional area of Africa has been home to several indigenous pre- colonial states and kingdoms since the second millennium BC, with the Nok civilization in the 15th century BC marking the first internal unification of the country. British influence and control over what would become Nigeria and Africa's most populous country grew through the 19th century. A series of constitutions after World War II granted Nigeria greater autonomy. After independence in 1960, politics were marked by coups and mostly military rule, until the death of a military head of state in 1998 allowed for a political transition. In 1999, a new constitution was adopted and a peaceful transition to civilian government was completed.

Nigeria is Sub Saharan Africa's largest economy and relies heavily on oil as its main source of foreign exchange earnings and government revenues. Its natural resources are natural gas, petroleum, tin, iron ore, coal, limestone, niobium, lead, zinc, and arable land.

Ethnic Groups
Nigeria is a multinational state inhabited by more than 250 ethnic groups. The three largest ethnic groups in the country alone make up around 60% of the total population of the country with 30% Hausa–Fulani in the north, 15.5% Yoruba in the west, and 15.2% Igbo in the east.

Some other most common ethnic groups are;

- ❖ Fulani 6%,
- ❖ Tiv 2.4%,
- ❖ Kanuri/Beriberi 2.4%,
- ❖ Ibibio 1.8%,
- ❖ Ijaw/Izon 1.8%, and other 24.7% (2018 est.)

Nigeria is divided almost in two parts with half of the Muslim population in the northern side and half of the Christian population in the southern region. The ratio of different religions in the country are as follows;

- ❖ Muslim 53.5%,
- ❖ Roman Catholic 10.6%,
- ❖ other Christian 35.3%,
- ❖ Other .6% (2018 est.)

Language
The official language of Nigeria is English facilitating the linguistic unity at national level. There are other 500 indigenous languages spoken in the country including Hausa, Yoruba, Igbo (Ibo), and Fulani.

Political Affiliation
Nigeria is a federal republic modeled after the United States, with executive power exercised by the President. The president is both chief of state, head of government, and commander-in-chief of the armed forces. The Federal Executive Council of the country is appointed by the president but is constrained constitutionally to include at least one member from each of the 36 states.

Contemporary Music

Fela Ransome Kuti

Born on 15th October 1938, Fela Ransome Kuti is a Nigerian musician and activist who launched a modern style of music called Afro-beat, which fused American blues, jazz, and funk with traditional Yoruba music. He was not only a musician but a multi-instrumentalist, a composer, political activist, bandleader, and Pan-Africanist. He was regarded as Africa's most challenging and charismatic music performer. He passed on August 2nd, 1997. He was also the founder of the Kalakuta Republic commune. The commune was built in 1970 and was destroyed in 1978 by the military of the Nigerian government.

Fela is considered the Father of Afrobeat. A musical term he created to engage the notions of Panafricanism dear to his mother, an early civil rights leader in Nigeria who opposed British rule during colonial times.

A keyboardist and saxophonist, Fela had one of the most electrifying bands of the continent and his concerts were mesmerizing. He has left an exceptional mark on African music and his genius as a composer showed the way forward to generations of young African musicians with respect to fusing various elements of African music and African cultures around the world. Felas's Afrobeat is a synthesis of African melodic, harmonic and call and response systems and aesthetics driven by the power of African rhythms.

His son Femi is keeping the torch alive.

King Sunny Ade

Born on 22nd September 1946, King Sunny Adé is a Nigerian jùjú singer, songwriter, and multi-instrumentalist. His real name is Chief Sunday Adeniyi Adegeye. Being recognized as the most influential singer of all the time, he is one of the first African pop musicians to gain international success. Sunny Adé formed his own band in 1967, African Beats. After achieving national success in Nigeria during the 1970s and founding his own independent label, Sunny Adé signed to Island Records in

1982 and achieved international success with the albums Juju Music (1982) and Synchro System (1983); the latter garnered him a Grammy nomination, a first for a Nigerian artist. His 1998 album Odu also garnered a Grammy nomination. He currently serves as chairperson of the Musical Copyright Society of Nigeria.

IK Dairo

Born in 1930 in the town of Offa, located in present-day Kwara State IK Dairo is one of the country's most famous juju musicians. His family was originally from Ijebu- Jesa before migrating to Offa. I.K. Dairo's musical career entered the fast lane when he founded a ten-piece band called the Morning Star Orchestra in 1957. Later in 1960, he was a part of lavish gatherings showcasing his patterns of Juju music celebrating the independence of Nigeria. He has released many songs however, 'Salome' and 'Ka Sora (Let Us Be Careful)', are his two big hits. Most of IK Dairo's music is a fusion of urban life and Yoruba culture. He is considered the Dean of the early Juju music of Nigeria.

Traditional music

Music of Yoruba

Yorùbá music is regarded as one of the more important components of the modern Nigerian popular music scene. It is traditionally centered on folklore and spiritual/deity worship, utilizing basic and natural instruments such as clapping of the hands. It is best known for its extremely advanced drumming tradition, especially using the dundun hourglass tension drums. The traditional Yoruba music was not influenced by foreign music. However, the modern-day Yoruba music has evolved and adapted itself through contact with foreign instruments and creativity.

Yoruba folk music was brought over to the Americas, North, Central and South by Africans during the era of the Atlantic Slave Trade. It became one of the most prominent West African cultural references and it has influenced every trend of Afro-Latin and Caribbean musical styles. Yoruba culture and spiritual rituals are very much alive in the North Eastern part of Brazil in Bahia as they shape the music and melodic systems expressed in Orisha worship used in Santería practices. This culture is also in evidence in the music and religious traditions of African worship and rituals in some parts of Louisiana, Alabama, Mississippi, Georgia in the United Sates and on the islands of Cuba, Haiti, Santo Domingo and everywhere else Africans went in the Caribbean.

Yoruba folk music became perhaps the most prominent kind of West African music in Afro-Latin and Caribbean musical styles; it left an especially important influence on the music used in Santería practice and the music of Cuba.

Igbo

Igbo music is the music of the Igbo people, who are indigenous to the southeastern part of Nigeria. Igbo Music incorporates a variety of musical styles. Some very popular styles are Igbo highlife, Igbo bongo, and Odumodu. The Igbo traditionally rely heavily on percussion instruments such as the drum and the gong, which are popular because of their innate ability to provide a diverse array of tempo, sound, and pitch. This type of music is generally lively, upbeat, and spontaneous creating variety of sounds enabling the Igbo people to incorporate music into almost all the facets of their daily lives.

Michael Babatunde Olatunji

Michael Babatunde Olatunji was born on 7th April 1927. He was a Nigerian drummer, recording artist, social activist, and educator by heart. He graduated from Morehouse College in 1954. Receiving a B.A. degree in Political Science with a minor in Sociology, he further went to New York University and enrolled in to the Public Administration and International Relations program. Olatunji's childhood was filled with singing and drumming. He has been known as the father of African drumming in the United States. He taught his fellow students some of the rhythms, songs, and dances of his native land. His first performance of African music and dance was organized in 1953.

For nearly fifty years, Olatunji has spread a message of love with his drum. In early 1960s, Olatunji rode a wave of popularity that earned him appearances on such programs as The Ed Sullivan Show, The Tonight Show with Johnny Carson, The Bell Telephone Hour, and The Mike Douglas Show. He had a deep connection with African American Jazz Icon John Coltrane who supported financially the Olatunji African Center in New York City for at the better part of a decade until his passing celebrated in his last recording entitled "Ogunde" Live at the Olatunji Center. Babatunde Olatunji passed April 6th, 2003.

Dr. Olatunji Euba

Olatunji Akin Euba was born in Lagos, Nigeria on 28th April 1935. Dr. Euba is a foremost composer, performer, and scholar of African art music. He was internationally known for pioneering the concepts of African Pianism, Intercultural Musicology, and Creative Ethnomusicology. He was also a member of the Yoruba ethnic group. His compositions involve a synthesis of African traditional music rooting from the ethnic groups and the Yoruba people infused with contemporary classical music. A musicology scholar

of great stature Dr. Euba, he held academic positions in London, Cambridge, Pittsburgh, PA and Beijing. His most ambitious composition is the opera Chaka: An Opera in Two Chants (1970). He also served as the head of music at the Nigerian Broadcasting Corporation. Dr. Euba passed on the 14th of April 2020.

Ghana

Ghana, officially the Republic of Ghana, is a country in West Africa. It spans along the Gulf of Guinea and the Atlantic Ocean, sharing borders with the Ivory Coast in the west, Burkina Faso in the north, Togo in the east, the Gulf of Guinea and the Atlantic Ocean in the south. Ghana covers an area of 238,535 km2 (92,099 sq mi), with a population of 32,372,889 (July 2021 est.).

The total land surface is around 227,533 sq km and the Water surface measures 11,000 sq km. It is the second-most populous country in West Africa, after Nigeria; and Accra is its capital and largest city. Formed from the merger of the British colony of the Gold Coast and the Togoland trust territory, Ghana in 1957 became the first Sub-Saharan country in colonial Africa to gain its independence.

Ghana is a multinational state, home to a variety of ethnic, linguistic and religious groups. According to the 2010 census, the vast majority, or 71.2%, of Ghana's population was Christian, 17.6% was Muslim, and 5.2% practised traditional faiths.

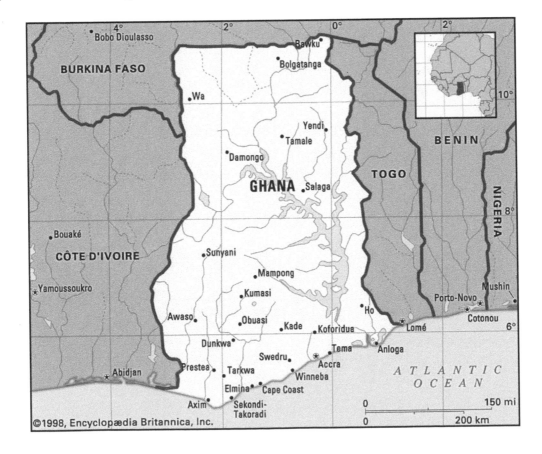

Ghana's diverse geography and ecology ranges from coastal savannahs to tropical rain forests. It is a unitary constitutional democracy led by a president who is both head of state and head of the government. Ghana's growing economic prosperity and democratic political system have increased its regional influence in West Africa.

Ghana is abundant is natural resources including gold, timber, industrial diamonds, bauxite, manganese, fish, rubber, hydropower, petroleum, silver, salt, and limestone. Ghana was a country of immigration in the early years after its 1957 independence, attracting labor migrants largely from Nigeria and other neighboring countries to mine minerals and harvest cocoa – immigrants composed about 12% of Ghana's population in 1960. In the late 1960s, worsening economic and social conditions discouraged immigration, and hundreds of thousands of immigrants, mostly Nigerians, were expelled.

During the 1970s, severe drought and an economic downturn transformed Ghana into a country of emigration; neighboring Cote d'Ivoire was the initial destination. Later, hundreds of thousands of Ghanaians migrated to Nigeria to work in its booming oil industry, but most were deported in 1983 and 1985 as oil prices plummeted.

Many Ghanaians then turned to more distant destinations, including other parts of Africa, Europe, and North America, but the majority continued to migrate within West Africa. Since the 1990s, increased emigration of skilled Ghanaians, especially to the US and the UK, drained the country of its health care and education professionals. Internally, poverty and other developmental disparities continue to drive Ghanaians from the north to the south, particularly to its urban centers.

Ghana is one of the emerging economies of West Africa and since the 1990s, increased movement of skilled Ghanaians to the US and the UK are draining the country of its health care and education professionals.

Ethnic Groups

The proportion of different ethnic groups within the country is as follows;

- ◆ Akan 47.5%, Mole-Dagbon 16.6%,
- ◆ Ewe 13.9%, Ga-Dangme 7.4%,
- ◆ Gurma 5.7%, Guan 3.7%, Grusi 2.5%,
- ◆ Mande 1.1%, other 1.4% (2010 est.).

However, Ghana also incorporates people from different religious backgrounds practicing different religions freely till date. The proportion is as follows; Christian 71.2% (Pentecostal/Charismatic 28.3%, Protestant 18.4%, Catholic 13.1%, other 11.4%), Muslim 17.6%, traditional 5.2%, other 0.8%, none 5.2% (2010 est.)

Languages

With English being the official language, there are more than 10 other languages spoken throughout the country including;

- ◆ Asante 16%, Ewe 14%, Fante 11.6%,
- ◆ Boron (Brong) 4.9%, Dagomba 4.4%,
- ◆ Dangme 4.2%, Dagarte (Dagaba) 3.9%,
- ◆ Kokomba 3.5%, Akyem 3.2%,
- ◆ Ga 3.1%, other 31.2% (2010 est.)

Political Affiliation

Ghana s a presidential republic type of government. The president is both chief of state and head of government. He reports to a parliamentary structure.

Contemporary Music

Emmanuel Tetteh Mensah

Emmanuel Tetteh Mensah was born on 31st May 1919 in Accra. E.T. hidden talent for music was discovered as early as in the school in Jamestown where he learned to read music and play the concert flute and piccolo. He was one the founding fathers of African popular music. In 1932, he joined the Accra Orchestra. His career stretched between 1936 to the late 1980s, and his music reached beyond Ghana to all corners of Africa and Europe.

Between 1936 and 1947, he worked with the Accra High School Orchestra, the Accra Rhythm Orchestra, the Kumasi Philharmonic Orchestra, and the Tempos. He later formulated two bands; E.T. Mensah and the Tempos and the Star Rockets. E.T. is widely famous for the composition of a highlife song entitled "Ghana Freedom Highlife" after the independence of Ghana. "The King of Highlife – African Rhythms" marks another great achievement. He passed on 19th July 1996.

Charles Kofi Amankwaa Mann

Charles Kofi Amankwaa Mann was born in 1936 in Cape Coast in the Central Region of Ghana. He was more commonly known as C. K. Mann. He was a former seaman who became the Ghanaian highlife musician and producer. Initially, He was a member of Moses Kwaku Oppong's Kakaiku's Guitar Band and later joined the Ocean Strings'. C. K. Mann's music career spanned over four decades. He also won multiple awards for his songs. He was awarded the Grand Medal of Ghana by John Agyekum Kufour in 2006. He passed on the 20th of March 2018.

King Bruce

King Bruce was born on 3rd June 1922 in in James Town, Accra,[3] Gold Coast (present-day Ghana). He was a Ghanaian composer, multi-instrumentalist, and band leader. He vividly made his mark on Ghana's dance band highlife tradition in a variety of ways. King learned the principles of Western music as well as songs from other Ghanaian ethnic groups in secondary school. He founded the black beats which he eventually handed to another group member after a success of six years. In 1970s, he got involved in organizing unions of musicians. In 1977, he returned to music after retiring from civil services and dedicated his home to teach other musicians. He passed on the 12th of September 1997.

Traditional Music
Music of Ghana

There are many styles of traditional and modern music of Ghana, due to Ghana's cosmopolitan geographic position on the African continent. The best known modern genre originating in Ghana is Highlife. For many years, Highlife was the preferred music genre until the introduction of Hiplife and many others. The northern musical traditions belong to the wider Sahelian musical traditions using stringed instruments such as the kologo lute and the gonjey fiddle, wind instruments such as flutes and horns, and

voice; with polyrhythms clapped or played on the talking drum, gourd drums or brekete bass drums. The music of the coast is associated with social functions, and relies on complex polyrhythmic patterns played by drums and bells as well as harmonized song.

Ghana's cosmopolitan geographic position on the African continent led it to benefit from a multiplicity of musical influences that shaped its modern genre called Highlife. Highlife was the most popular music genre until the introduction of Hiplife. The northern musical traditions belong to the wider Sahelian musical traditions using stringed instruments such as the kologo lute and the gonjey fiddle, wind instruments such as flutes and horns, and voice; with polyrhythms clapped or played on the talking drum, gourd drums or brekete bass drums. The musical traditions, rhythmic vocabulary and expressions of the talking drum are a science unto themselves. They have given birth to an enormous vocabulary of textures and tonal colors that Western ethnomusicologists have yet to fully appreciate. The celebrated Oxford trained Ghanaian ethnomusicologist Dr. Koffi Agawu has written extensive essays on the complexities and the depth of talking drum music and its textural palettes.

Chapter 6

North Africa; Morocco, Algeria, Egypt, Sudan

Morocco

Morocco is a mountainous country of western North Africa that lies directly across the Strait of Gibraltar from Spain. The total area of Morocco is 715, 550 sq. km of which 716,300 sq. km is land. The climate is Mediterranean in the North and becomes hotter and dryer in the South. Natural resources of Morocco include phosphates, iron ore, manganese, lead, zinc, fish, and salt.

The population of Morocco is 36,561,813 according to 2021 census. There is a demographic transition that has been taking place in the country. The population of Morocco is growing at a declining rate. The fertility rate is coming down owing to family awareness in women and better approach to contraceptive. During the second half of the 20th century, Morocco was one of the top countries in terms of emigration which was encouraged by the government as well to grow remittances. According to 2021 estimates the population growth rate of Morocco is 0.92%.

The capital of Morocco is Rabat whose name is derived from Ribat el-Fath that means stronghold of victory. The literacy rate of Morocco is

73.8 with the urban population of 63.5%. The GDP per Capita of Morocco is 8,600$.

Morocco is a constitutional monarchy with two legislative houses. According to the constitution promulgated in 2011, political power in Morocco is to be shared between the hereditary monarch and an elected bicameral parliament, consisting of the House of Councilors and the House of Representatives. Currently, King Mohamed VI is the Chief of the State. Exiled by French colonial forces his grandfather King Mohamed V successfully wrestled his country from the French government in 1956. King Mohamed V's son Hassan II

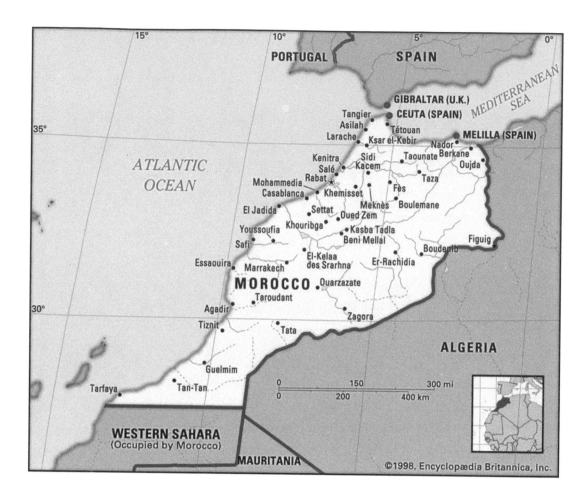

was a scholar committed to Africa, and one who undertook an immense economic and artistic effort that culminated in making the country of Morocco an economic power in North Africa and one of the best representatives of what religious and cultural tolerance should look like between Muslims, Jews and Christians in Africa.

Ethnic Groups

Racial and religious demographics;

- Arabs 30%
- Berbers 60%
- West Africans of Malian origin 10%
- 98% Sunni Muslims
- 2% Christian, Jewish, and Baha'i.
- Jews are about 6000 as per 2010 census.

Languages

Arabic and Tamazight and Berber are the three official languages of the country with French being a corporate language. French is usually spoken in business and governmental dealing.

Morocco is a constitutional monarchy with a parliamentary system.

Contemporary Music

Hassan Hakmoun

Hassan Hakmoun was born on 16th September 1963 in a Gnawa musical family. Hassan plays the Sintir, the Moroccan three-stringed bass, and many of his songs have the Gnawa's eternal, nomadic quality. By the age of fourteen, he was a well-known musician performing at Gnawa lila ceremonies with his own group in Morocco. Hassan Hakmoun is one of the great ambassadors of Gnawa music abroad. In New York, Hakmoun began to enlarge his musical palette adding American textural colors to Gnawa music while always maintaining the roots of authenticity of this unique North African musical Moroccan form born. He formed the group Zahar, meaning 'luck', whose music incorporated elements of rock and Jazz with African styles. His albums topped the charts for World Music Albums, World Music Charts Europe, New World and CMJ's Radio Top 150.

Traditional Music

Gnawa Music

Historically, Gnawa music was brought by populations from Mali to Morocco. It has maintained its repertoire of sub-Saharan melodic, harmonic and complex polyrhythmic systems inducing meditation and trances. It is a well-preserved heritage merging ritual poetry with traditional music and dancing. The music is executed at lila, (communal nights of celebration devoted to prayer and healing) led by the Gnawa maalem, or master musician, and their group of musicians and dancers. Gnawa music has spread to numerous other nations in Africa, Europe, and the United States. One of its ardent supporters was the celebrated African American NEA Jazz Master, composer, and pianist Randy Weston who operated a Jazz venue in Tangiers and made a study of the culture and the music of the Gnawa with maalem master Abdallah El Gourd.

The melodic language of the Sintir of the Gnawa (stringed instrument) is closely connected to the vocals and to the rhythms of the speech patterns, as in most African music concepts. Its instrumentation includes large, heavy iron castanets identified as krakebs and a three-string lute known as a Hajhuj, Gimbri, or Sintir. The textural combination of these two instruments is essential to the tonal expression of Gnawa music. The polyrhythms of Gnawa music are anchored in the genial 6/8 polyrhythmic systems of Malian expression and are trance inducing. The sacred rituals of the music and its spiritual medicinal properties continue to remain hidden and safeguarded from the public by its progenitors.

Mahmoud Guinia

Born in 1951 in the city Essaouira on the Atlantic coast, Mahmoud Guinia was one of Morocco's most sought after master Gnawa singer and Guimbri player. He recorded for both domestic and foreign labels, and collaborated with numerous western musicians. The Shaman of the Sahara music recordings were released in 2001 with Maallem Mahmoud Guinia in partnership with Tata Guines, Victor Vidal Paz and various Indonesian musicians. He was the authentic repository of an entire Gnawa culture and his live recordings continue to be a testimony of the strength of his traditions and the mastery of his instrumental and vocal performances His album titled Colours of the Night is a required listen. Master Guinia passed on 2nd August 2015. His legacy and the traditions of excellence and authenticity live on through his sons, most notably Maallem Houssam Guinia.

Zohra Al Fassiya

Zohra Al Fassiya was a Jewish singer and poet from Morocco, born in 1905 in Sefrou. Considered one of the queens of the melhoun and gharnati genres, she is one of the pioneers of modern Arabic music in North Africa. She started singing at a very young age when performing religious songs at her synagogue.

In the 1940s, she led her an orchestra and wrote her own songs. She was heavily aired on radio stations, both in Morocco and Algeria, and was enormously well known and adored by the public In 1962, Al Fassiya relocated in Israel where her more traditional vocal talent and music were only and mostly recognized within the Moroccan community of Israel. As a result her career faded way too soon. Zohra Al Fassiya passed at the age 89 in 1994 and was buried in Israel.

Algeria

Algeria is located in Northern Africa. The country borders the Mediterranean Sea and lies between Morocco and Tunisia. The neighboring countries are Libya, Mali, Mauritania, Morocco, Niger, and Tunisia. The terrain is typically high plateau and desert. The main natural resources include petroleum, natural gas, iron ore, phosphates, uranium, lead, zinc. The climate of Algeria is arid to semiarid. Along the coast the climate is dry and there are hot summers. On high plateaus, where the climate is dry as well, winters are cold and the summers are hot.

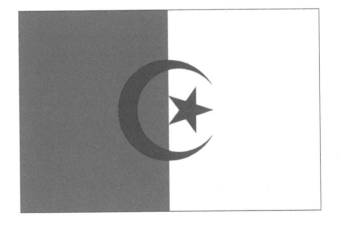

The population of Algeria is 43,576,691. The population growth rate of Algeria is 1.52%. Literacy rate in Algeria is 81.4%. And 73.7% of the total population lives in urban settings. Its Capital is Algiers.

Historically, Algeria has known many empires and dynasties starting with the ancient Numidians or Moors (3rd century B.C.), Phoenicians, Carthaginians, Romans, Vandals, Byzantines, over a dozen different Arab and Berber dynasties, Spaniards, and Ottoman Turks. It was under the latter that the Barbary pirates operated from North Africa and preyed on shipping beginning in roughly 1500, peaking in the early to mid-17th century, until finally subdued by the French capture of Algiers in 1830. The French southward conquest of the entirety of Algeria proceeded throughout the 19th century and was marked by many atrocities. The country was colonized by the

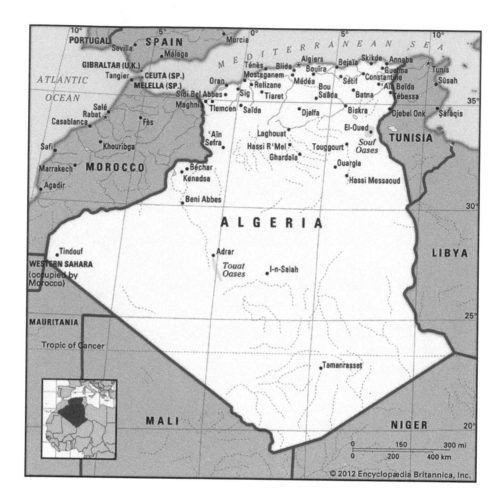

French in the late 19th and early 20th centuries. A bloody eight-year struggle culminated in Algerian independence in 1962 with the help of Cuban Special Forces.

Algeria's economy remains dominated by the state, a legacy of the country's socialist post-independence development model. Hydrocarbons have long been the backbone of the economy, accounting for roughly 30% of GDP.

Ethnic Groups
Similar to Morocco, Algeria is also home to only one major ethnic group;

- Arabs, Berbers and Kabyles 99%
- Europeans 1%

Algeria is mostly a muslin country with 99% presence of Muslim Sunnis and only 1% Christians and Jews.

Languages
With Arabic and Tamazight/Berber being the official languages spoken in the region there are a few languages spoken as well they are;

- Kabyle Berber (Taqbaylit)
- Shawiya Berber (Tacawit)
- Mzab Berber
- Tuareg Berber (Tamahaq)

It is a constitutional republic with a president and a representative assembly.

Contemporary Music

Khaled Ibrahim

Khaled, who is recognized as Cheb Khaled was born on 29th February, 1960 in Oran, Algeria. He is credited with propelling to Western audiences a cultural and musical form called Rai. It is a traditional form of secular Algerian popular music expressing the hardships and hopes of its working class communities. Eminently talented he records his first single, "La Route du Lycée" ("The Road to School") as a teenager. His ability to synthesize many musical genres with the addition of modern instrumentation to the service of his unique textural vocal expression made him the uncontested leader of the genre in the 1990s in Europe and in the Arab world. His collaborations with other talented Rai artists such as Rachid Taha, and Faudel are enshrined in the documentary concert entitled the "3 Soleils".

Rachid Taha

Rachid Taha, born on 18th September 1958 in a small village outside the port city of Oran on Algeria's sea coast, was an Algerian singer and activist based in France. While significantly rooted in the Rai expression and culture of his native country his musical interests were varied and his music reflected that sonic and textural curiosity which encompassed many different styles including rock, electronic, and punk. Immigrating to France at the age of 10 with his family, his story reflects the complexities associated with the frictions of cultural identity unease connected to the realities of growing up a foreigner from North Africa in a European country. His cover of Charles Trenet's song entitled Douce France (Sweet France) was the beginning of his career and the confirmation of his status as a vocalist with a social consciousness. His work with producer Steve Hillage (formerly of the psychedelic band Gong) would propel him to international celebrity. Subsequently, Hillage would produce most of Taha's albums, the anthemic anti-racism gem Voila Voila in 1993, Ole Ole in 1995 and Diwan in 1999. Rachid Taha passed suddenly September 12, 2018 in Paris.

Cheb Mami

Mohamed Khelifati, whose stage name is Cheb Mami, was born on 11th July 1966, is an Algerian musician and singer-songwriter. He sings and speaks in Algerian Arabic and sometimes in French or Eastern Arabic dialects. He is

one of the prodigious voices of North Africa and a show stopping entertainer. In 1985, Mami came to Paris and found his musical niche. His music is a blend of Mediterranean and Western influences as well as Latin music. His vocal power is supreme and he is a skilled accordionist. His collaboration with British rocker Sting on the album Brand New Day was released in 1999, and his duet, "Desert Rose" toppled the singles charts worldwide.

Traditional Music

Cheikha Rimitti

Cheikha Rimitti, born in May 1923, was considered the Dean of Algerian Rai music. At 15, she joined a company of traditional Algerian musicians and learnt to sing and dance. In 1943 she moved to the town of Relizane in the rural area of the country and began writing her own songs. They described the life of the Algerian poor, the struggle of living, the pleasures of sex, love, alcohol and friendship and the harsh realities of war. Rimitti was one of the first to sing songs of lust in public and did so in the earthy language of the street. She ultimately composed over 200 songs. Her opinions and choice of texts did not endear her to the nationalist forces fighting for freedom from French rule during the Algerian War of Independence and she was censured for singing a folklore perverted by colonialism. In the 1980s, Cheikha Rimitti moved to Paris. Her music crossed over to the Europe and she undertook prestigious concerts worldwide. She passed in Paris from a heart attack on 15 May 2006, aged 83.

Egypt

Egypt is situated in North Eastern piece of Africa, lining the Mediterranean Sea, among Libya and the Gaza Strip, and the Red Sea north of Sudan, and incorporates the Asian Sinai Peninsula. Its geological directions are 27 00 N, 30 00 E. The absolute area of Egypt is 1,001,450sq km. The territory of Egypt is huge desert level hindered by Nile valley and delta. The normal assets that are found in Egypt incorporate petrol, petroleum gas, iron metal, phosphates, manganese, limestone, gypsum, powder, asbestos, lead, uncommon earth components, and zinc.

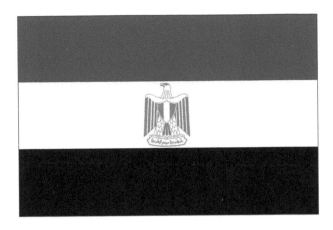

Western geo-political and strategic interests in Africa have successfully enrolled academia and the press in distilling the confusing notion to the rest of the planet that may be Egypt should reside in a place called the Middle East instead of Africa.

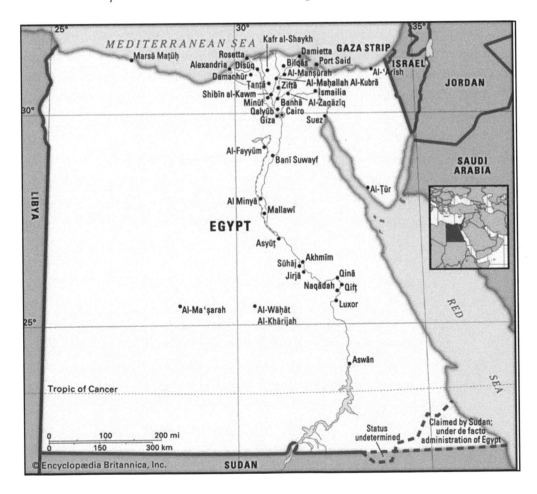

This academic canard is an effort to pull the immense cultural legacies of the Black civilizations of Nubia and Egypt who built the pyramids away from the African continent, in an effort to satisfy the nonsensical colonial mentality of academic White supremacy engaged in the Hollywood driven dashed hopes of making Egypt and its African civilizations somewhat parts of an absurd and comical European cultural community, hence the financing of Liz Taylor as Cleopatra, Pharoah of Egypt.

The total population of Egypt is 106,437,241. Most of the country is desert, so about 95% of the population is concentrated in a narrow strip of fertile land along the Nile River, which represents only about 5% of Egypt's land area. Egypt's rapid population growth, which was 46% between the 20 years from 1994-2014, has put a major strain on natural resources, jobs, housing, sanitation, education, and health care. About 42.8% of the total population lives in urban areas. The capital of Egypt is Cairo.

In the 13th century, a local military caste, the Mamluks took control and continued to govern even after the conquest of Egypt by the Ottoman Turks in 1517. Opening the Red Sea to the Mediterranean, the completion of the Suez Canal in 1869 elevated Egypt as an important world transportation hub. Ostensibly to protect its investments, Britain seized control of Egypt's government in 1882, but nominal allegiance to the Ottoman Empire continued until 1914. Partially independent from the UK in 1922, Egypt acquired full sovereignty from Britain in 1952 under the leadership of its first President Gamal Abdel Nasser.

Egypt is a Republic with multi party representation.

Ethnic Groups

The Egyptian Copts are the majority ethnic group followed by Berbers. The Nubians are clustered along the Nile in the southern part of the country.

The religious demographics show 90% Sunni Muslims and 10% Christians. Christians are subdivided in different groups; with a majority Coptic, Orthodox, Armenian Apostolic, Catholic, Maronite, and Anglican.

Languages

Arabic is the official language of Egypt. Besides Arabic, English and French are also spoken and understood.

Contemporary Music

Umm Kulthum

Umm Kulthum, born on 4th May 1904, was an Egyptian singer who enthralled African and Arab audiences worldwide for half a century. She was recognized as the African Diva of Arabic expression and one of the most powerful voices ever heard in the 20th century. She is with Mahalia Jackson, and Maria Callas one of the defining voices of the mid-20th century.

Umm Kulthum came from very modest beginnings. Her father was a Cheikh (Teacher of the Koran) and she learned to enunciate perfectly at a very young age. The power of her vocals, her constant attention to diction coupled

with the high aesthetics of the lyrics she sung allowed her to tower over all others in the genre. Um Kulthum was a diva who understood the power of the image better than most. She lived a life of great discretion preferring her fans not know about her daily activities and she maintained an aura of mystery all of her life. She was a fervent patriot who raised money for the war effort of her nation against Israel. Her weekly radio program had a reach that extended from North Africa, the Arab world to the Soviet Union Republics. Um Kulthum became a cultural icon. In 2001, the Egyptian government created the Kawkab al-Sharq Museum of Cairo to celebrate her life and accomplishments. She passed on February 3rd, 1975 and continues to remain one of the best selling African vocalists of Arabic culture, decades after her death.

Umm Kulthum

Mohamed Abdel Wahab

Mohamed Abdel Wahab was born in 1902 in Cairo, Egypt. A child prodigy he began his singing career at age 13 and made his first recording. Always very attentive to technology and the role of technology in the dissemination of culture Abdel Wahab enters the world of movies and musical films after visiting Paris and watching musicals there. He introduces the musicals in film in Egypt in 1933 to a resounding success. His film the White Flower broke all box offices records. In 1950, he returns to singing. A prolific composer he pens more than 1800 songs laying the foundation for a new Egyptian music using the Nubian ould. Always open to outside influences he introduces the waltz and rocknroll rhythms into Egyptian music and gets criticized for it to no avail. As a composer he writes songs for Um Kulthum, Lebanese icon Fairuz and accompanies on the ould the poet Ahmed Shakwi. Mohamed Abdel Wahab is the

champion of modern Egyptian music. He has left an immense musical legacy and a statue of him was erected in his native neighborhood. He passed in Cairo May 4, 1992.

Traditional Music

Music of Egypt

Music has been an essential part of Egyptian culture since ancient times in Egypt. Music was always associated with sciences and mathematics in Egyptian Antiquity and in Nubian Antiquity before that. There are treatises about musical rules of harmony and their impact on human health on papyrus. Depictions in the pyramids of the harps and banjo like string instruments define the notions of a high culture and civilization attentive to the influence of the sonic landscape associated with the health and wellbeing of humans in general. Egyptian music and culture born out of Sub Saharan and Nubian culture and civilization is the foundation of Greek culture therefore European culture through the Romans.

Chronology, chronology, chronology, (I keep having to come back again and again to this concept) the existence of Nubia and Egypt as civilizational centers predate the Greeks by more than 4000 years. The Greeks who studied in Egypt owe the entirety of their civilizational foundation, science, arts and culture to Africa, Nubia and Egypt in particular (Freud, 1939) which is why its most celebrated Emperor namely, Alexander the Great did not build his capital in Athens or Macedonia but in Alexandria, Egypt, why? Because Nubia and Egypt were the center of world civilizations, science, state management, military strategy and arts combined under the watchful eye of the 10,000 years old Sphynx built at a time when Europe was just emerging from the Ice Age.

The mathematics of African tonalities are inscribed on the stone walls of the pyramids (Lubicz, 1957). The rules of scale systems organizing the length of the strings' sizes of the harp are established thousands of years before Pythagoras comes to study in Egypt as evidenced by the paintings inside pyramids that were completed thousands of years before Pythagoras

was born, so we should stop talking about the "Western tempered scale" or the diatonic scale or pentatonic systems as if these were Western discoveries for they were not. From Kora harp like instruments to balafon xylophone like instruments, Africans, Nubians, and Egyptians were playing complex and sophisticated string, wind and percussion instruments with elaborate dance choreographies before Europe had any musical instruments of its own.

The reality is that in Antiquity until the downfall of the Roman Empire all the musical instruments of the Greeks, the Hebrews, and the Romans came from African conception, traditions and civilization without exception. The well recognized Greek Lyre in the hands of many Greek sculptures and paintings is in fact the Niatiti of Kenya why? Because the Luos (ethnic group of Kenya) were playing music and were playing the Niatiti on the planet thousands of years before the Greeks even existed. It is not a Greek Lyre, it is a Luo Niatiti borrowed by the Greeks from these

Kenyan populations who were the first on the planet and this goes on and on…

Middle Eastern music is born out of the fundamentals of Nubian and Egyptian music. The concept of Western musical modes comes from the tonometric established musical systems of the various African civilizations and populations who dominated that part of the world over the centuries before the Greeks. It is a well-established fact that pentatonic, diatonic, heptatonic, microtonic tonal systems existed in sub Saharan Africa and in Nubia predating the Greeks by thousands of years of existence so why do we keep calling these tonal systems by the European Greek term "pentatonic" (a term from a group of people i.e. the Greeks who did not create any of these tonal systems). Shouldn't we instead of using a foreign Greek term such as "pentatonic" propose an African term? Isn't it true that any African term would be closer in origin than that of a Greek word which has no cultural relevance whatsoever to the music of African people? The conversation about whether rules of harmony are a European invention becomes even more non-sensical given that Africans were the first to have created a fixed tonality instrument i.e. balafon or xylophone. Can you seriously build a fixed tone instrument such as a balafon without creating the first rules of harmony for the rest of the planet to borrow? Once you have cut the blade of wood to a certain dimension which gives you a fixed tonality when you hit it you need to define an aesthetic of tonality i.e. harmony to cut the dimension of the next blade of wood that you will affix next to it thus engendering what? You guessed it, rules of harmony because these tones are created to be played simultaneously. Unlike string instruments which are melodically and harmonically unstable by the nature of their media i.e. strings, fixed tone instruments in wood such as the balafon do not deviate in tonometry thus cementing and defining a concept of rules of harmony in these African population groups long, long before Europe.

◇◇

North Sudan & South Sudan

Sudan is located in the south of the north-eastern part of Africa, bordering the Red Sea, between Egypt and Eritrea. The total area of Sudan is 1,861,484 sq km. The border countries to Sudan include Central African Republic, Chad, Egypt, Eritrea, Ethiopia, Libya, and South Sudan. The climate of Sudan is hot and dry and the terrain is generally flat. The natural resources include petroleum; small reserves of iron ore, copper, chromium ore, zinc, tungsten, mica, silver, gold; hydropower.

Sudan is home to a population of 46,751,152 people according to 2021 census. With this massive number of people living under the flag of Sudan, 35.6% of the total population is Urban Population. The rate of population growth in the country is estimated to be 2.69%.

Egyptian occupation early in the 19th century was overthrown by a native Mahdist Sudan state (1885-99) that was crushed by the British who then set up an Anglo-Egyptian Sudan, in effect a British colony. Following independence from Anglo-Egyptian co-rule in 1956, military regimes favoring Islamic-oriented governments have dominated national politics. Sudan was embroiled in two prolonged civil wars during most of the remainder of the 20th century. This conflict resulted in the partitioning of Sudan into two states.

Sudan has experienced protracted social conflict and the loss of three quarters of its oil production due to the secession of South Sudan. The oil sector had driven much of Sudan's GDP growth since 1999. The interruption of oil production in South Sudan in 2012 for over a year and the consequent loss of oil transit fees further exacerbated the fragile state of Sudan's economy.

Ethnic Groups

African Sudanese form around 70% of Sudan's population. 30% comes under the following ethnic groups;

◈ Fur, Beja, Nuba & Fallata

Sudan is mostly a Sunni Muslim country with Christians present in minority.

Languages

Arabic and English are the official languages of Sudan. Other languages include:

◈ Nubian – TaBedawie - Fur

North Sudan with its flag and capital at Khartoum

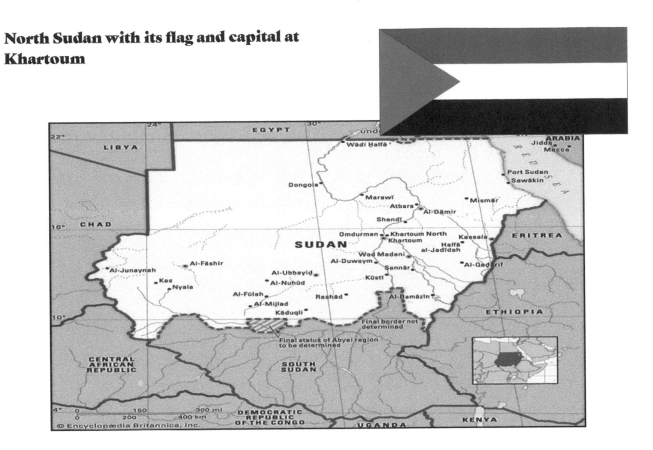

South Sudan with its flag and capital at Juba.

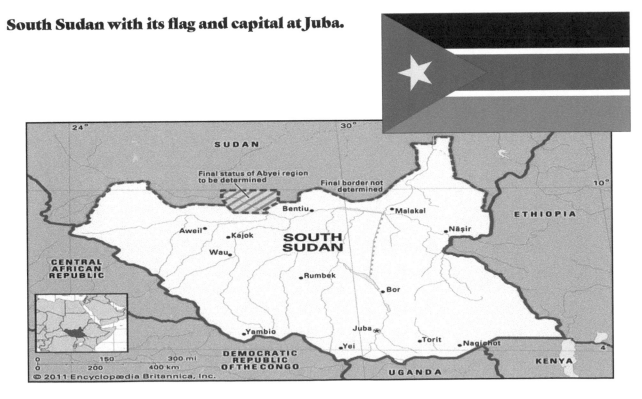

Traditional Music

Hamza El Din

Hamza El Din was born on 10th July 1929 in southern Egypt. He was an Egyptian composer, vocalist, and an oud and tar player. He studied the music of his native region Nubia, near the Egypt–Sudan border. He subsequently lived and studied in Italy, Japan, and the United States.

El Din played the oud, a Nubian instrument. His virtuoso performances attracted the attention of the Grateful Dead, Joan Baez, and Bob Dylan in the 1960s, which led to a recording contract and to his eventual relocation to the United States. Following his appearance at the Newport Folk Festival in 1964, he recorded two albums for Vanguard Records, released 1964–65. His 1971 recording Escalay The Water Wheel (published by Nonesuch Records) is recognized as one of the first world music recordings to gain wide release in the West. He also performed with the Grateful Dead, most famously during their Egypt concerts of 1978. His defining album was entitled "Eclipse". Hamza El Din was one of the most recognized ambassadors of Nubian/Sudanese music and culture worldwide. He passed on the 22nd of May 2006 in Berkeley, California.

Chapter 7

East Africa; Ethiopia, Kenya, Uganda, Tanzania, Mozambique

Ethiopia

Located in the Eastern portion of Africa, west of Somalia, its surface area is 1,104,300 sq km. The climate is typically tropical with wide variation based on altitude. It is a very mountainous country. It is rich in natural resources, gold, platinum, copper, potash, natural gas, and hydropower. Addis Ababa (which means New Flower) is the Capital.

With a population estimated to be 108.4 million, its growth rate is found to be 2.83 %. 21% of its population lives in urban areas. Its greater majority is employed in agriculture.

Unique among African countries, the ancient Ethiopian monarchy maintained its freedom from colonial rule with the exception of a short-lived Italian occupation from 1936-41. It shifted from a monarchy to a socialist republic in 1974 and returned to a constitutional republic with multi party representation in 1994.

Ethiopia has been home to all three major religions, Judaism, Christianity and Islam. It has been a home for Judaism and Orthodox Christianity from the very beginning of these two religions and

the mountains of Ethiopia have provided a sanctuary for the peaceful evolution of these two religions and their worshippers.

Ethnic Groups

Several ethnic groups in Ethiopia:

Oromo 34.9%, Amhara (Amara) 27.9%, Tigray (Tigrinya) 7.3%, Sidama 4.1%, Welaita 3%, Gurage 2.8%, Somali (Somalia) 2.7%, Hadiya 2.2%, Afar (Affar) .6%, Other 12.6%.

The religions are; Ethiopian Orthodox 43.8%, Muslim 31.3%, Protestant 22.8%, Catholic 0.7%, Animists .6%, Other 0.8%

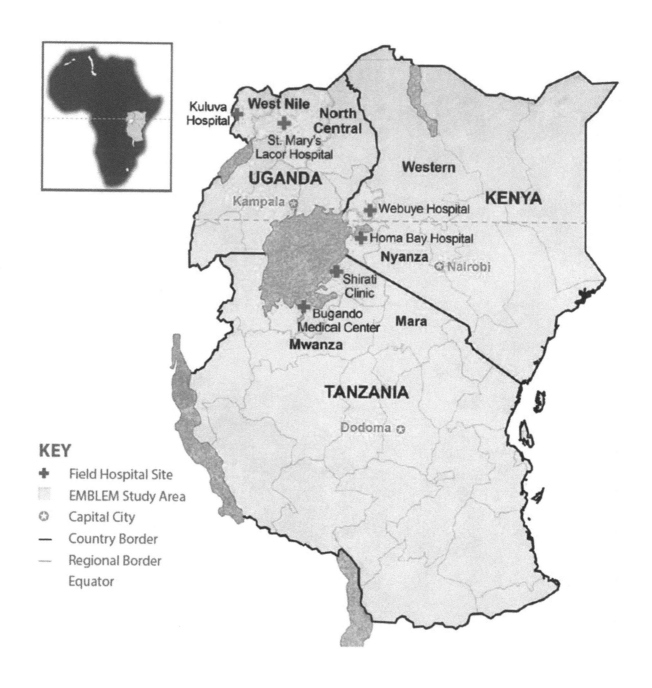

KEY

✚ Field Hospital Site

▨ EMBLEM Study Area

✪ Capital City

— Country Border

— Regional Border

Equator

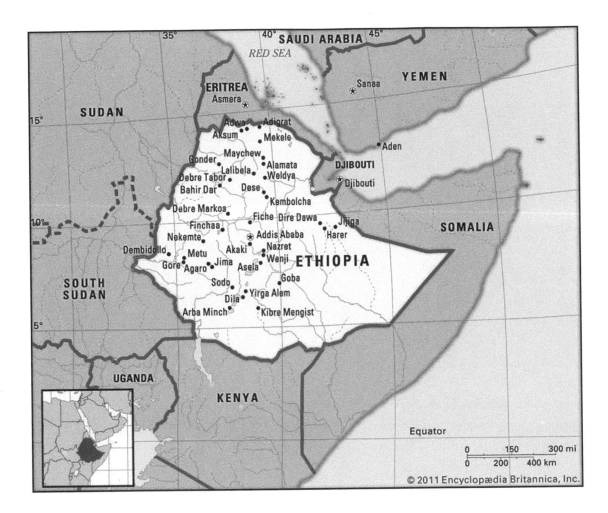

Languages

Amharic is the official National Language; whereas, different states have different official working languages. English is the major foreign language taught in schools. Following languages are spoken in Ethiopia:

Oromo 33.8%, Amharic 29.3%, Somali 6.2%, Tigrigna (Tigrinya) 5.9%, Sidamo 4%, Wolaytta 2.2%, Gurage 2%, Afar 1.7%, Hadiyya 1.7%, Gamo 1.5% , Gedeo 1.3%, Opuuo 1.2%, Kafa 1%, Other 8.1%.

Ethiopia is a constitutional republic with multiparty representation.

Contemporary Music

Aster Aweke

Born in 1958 in Gondar, Ethiopia, Aster Aweke is one of the standard bearers of the newer generation of Ethiopian singers. Aster's voice has been dubbed "The Voice of Ethiopia". She gained worldwide recognition and fame for her 1999 album Hagere, and her 2008 album Fikir.

Aster Aweke

At an early age, she began performing in clubs and hotels in the capital with bands such as the Continental Band, Hotel D'Afrique Band, Shebele Band and Ibex Band.

Disillusioned by the local politics at home, she moved to the United States in 1981. Returning to Ethiopia in 1997, she performed in Addis Ababa for a crowd of over 50,000 people. She is a star who uses her platform to raise funds for relief and school initiatives all over Ethiopia.

Mahmoud Ahmed

Mahmoud Ahmed was born May 8th 1941 in Addis Ababa. He is an Ethiopian singer of Gurage lineage. He gained great fame in Ethiopia in the 1970s and among the Ethiopian diaspora in the 1980s. He is recognized as one of the most important musicians and vocalists of Africa and his unique ability to infuse traditional East African melodic and rhythmic systems with American Jazz has been a model for African composers worldwide.

After recording his first single with the Venus Band "Nafqot New Yegodagn" and "Yasdestal" in 1971, Mahmoud continued to work with several bands for the Amha and Kaifa record labels throughout the 1970s. In the 1980s, Mahmoud had his own music store in Addis Ababa's Piazza district while keeping up with his singing career. He became one of the first modern Ethiopian musicians to perform in the United States with a 1980–1981 tour with the Walias Band, Getatchew Kassa, and Webeshet Fisseha. In 1986, the Belgian label Crammed Discs released his collection entitled "Ere Mela Mela" drawn from two LPs which Mahmoud had recorded in Addis Ababa with the Ibex Band a decade earlier which brought him immediate international recognition.

More international popularity surged in the late 1990s after Buda Musique promoted the Éthiopiques series on compact disc. He still tours internationally, performing concerts both for world music fans as well as the Ethiopian diaspora. In 2007, Mahmoud won the BBC World Music Award.

Traditional Music

Alemu Aga

Alemu Aga, born near Addis Ababa in 1950, is an Ethiopian musician, singer, and master of the traditional musical string instrument of the Ethiopian Orthodox Church called the Begena. The 10 string instrument is an East African harp similar to those depicted in the Egyptian pyramids three thousand years ago. Alemu was a student of the celebrated Begena master Aleqa Tessema.

Alemu majored in Earth Sciences at the University of Addis Ababa but continued to practice and perform the Begena at religious ceremonies and cultural events. He became a music professor at the Yared School of Music.

Recognized by UNESCO in 1972, his musical work was recorded and preserved as one of the important cultural elements of Ethiopian heritage. He has since been acknowledged worldwide as one of the pre-eminent masters of this ancient Christian celebrated musical tradition.

His 1995 musical collaboration entitled "Ende Jerusalem" with Krar master player Asnakech Worku received rave reviews nationally and internationally. The album "The Harp of King David" was released in 2009.

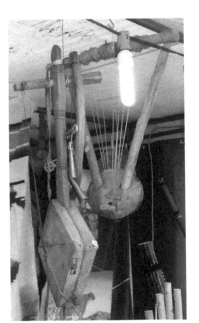

Music of Ethiopia

Ethiopian music is a term that can mean any music of Ethiopian origin. It has a distinct melodic modal system inclusive of long intervals between notes.

The music of the Ethiopian Highlands tends to use modal scale systems called qenet (or genre). There are four dominant modes: tezeta, bati, ambassel, and anchihoy. Three additional modes exist and represent variations on the above: tezeta minor, bati major, and bati minor. Certain songs are named after their qenet, such as tizita, which is a song of reminiscence.

In the Ethiopian highlands the music can be either monophonic or heterophonic. In certain areas of the South, the music is polyphonic. Dorze polyphonic singing or (edho) may employ up to five parts; Majangir, four parts. Rhythmically, the polyrhythmic concept of 6/8 tends to be preferred.

Kenya

Located in Eastern Africa, Kenya borders the Indian Ocean, between Somalia and Tanzania. The surface area of Kenya is 580,367 sq km. Its climate varies from tropical along coast to arid in interior. Its natural resources are limestone, soda ash, salt, gemstones, fluorspar, zinc, diatomite, gypsum, wildlife, and hydropower. Its capital is Nairobi, which means in the indigenous language Masai "the place of cool waters".

Population of Kenya is 48.4 million. 27% of the total population is urban population. It has a population growth rate of 1.57%. GDP per capita in Kenya is 3,500$ according to the 2017 estimates.

It is a constitutional republic with multi party representation, independent since 1963.

Kenya is East Africa's economic, financial, and transport powerhouse with an economic growth averaging over 5% for the last decade.

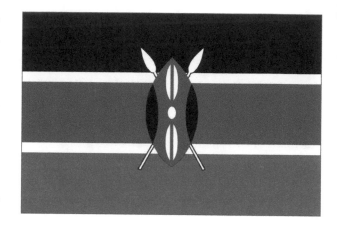

Ethnic Groups

The main ethnic groups of Kenya are:

Kikuyu 17.1%, Luhya 14.3%, Kalenjin 13.4%, Luo 10.7%, Kamba 9.8%, Somali 5.8%, Kisii 5.7%, Mijikenda 5.2%, Meru 4.2%, Masai 2.5%, Turkana 2.1%, Non-Kenyan 1%, Other 8.2%

The greater majority of population is Christian. Islam is the second most popular religion.

Christian 85.5% (Protestant 33.4%, Catholic 20.6%, Evangelical 20.4%, African Instituted Churches 7%, other Christian 4.1%, Muslim 10.9%, Other 1.8%, Animist 1.6%

Languages

English and Kiswahili are the official languages. In addition, there are many indigenous languages.

It is a constitutional republic with multi party representation.

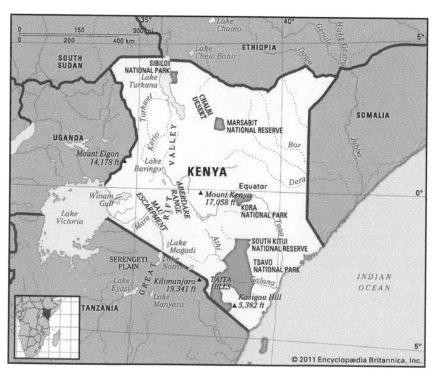

Contemporary Music

Daniel Misiani

Daniel Owino Misiani was born on 22nd February 1940 in in Nyamagongo, Tanzania. He was a Tanzanian-born musician based in Kenya, where he led the Shirati Jazz collective. He was known as "the Godfather of the Benga musical style ", which he pioneered. His parents were singers, but frowned upon his choice of a musical career on religious grounds. He moved to Kenya in the 1960s to be a musician. He first recorded with the Victoria Boys in 1965. The band changed its name several times before becoming popular as Shirati Jazz band. Daniel sang most-

ly in Dholuo and Swahili languages. He was a gifted guitarist whose intricate floating and contrapuntal melodic lines left his audiences baffled and dancing. A politically engaged musician he found himself in prison a few times for singing lyrics that had been deemed subversive. The Godfather of Benga music, Daniel Misiani passed at the age of 66 on May 17, 2006 in a road accident. His wife and long-time band member Queen Babito continued performing his musical legacy.

Winyo

Born Shiphton Onyango, Winyo adopted his artistic name 'Winyo', which is a Luo word (a tribe from the Lake Victoria region of Western Kenya) for "a bird". The reason for this becomes apparent once you hear him sing. His melodic voice has been linked to that of a singing bird. Immensely gifted the guitarist/vocalist Winyo's music is a contemporary stylistic rendition of the Benga style of Kenya. He sings in Dholuo, Swahili and English, and remains committed to speaking about social issues involving child poverty, and homelessness. He has received numerous world music awards and recognition and even recorded with Brazilian musical giant Gilberto Gil during his visit to Rio de Janeiro.

Job Seda or artist name Ayub Ogada

Ayub Ogada was born in 1956 in Mombasa, Kenya. He is Luo and was influenced by the musical heritage of his parents who were musicians. They performed

Luo music to Kenyan and US audiences. Ayub's experience of travelling with his parents to the US and his exposure to both western and African cultures had a profound effect on his music and perspectives.

Traveling to London, he was approached and asked to perform at the Womad Music. British rock star Peter Gabriel noticed him and Ayub was invited to record and perform with him. In 1993, he recorded his first album En Mana Kuoyo (Just Sand) at Peter Gabriel's studion and began touring extensively.

Ayub's music is on the soundtracks of films such as I Dreamed of Africa (2000), The Constant Gardener (2005), Samsara (2011) and The Good Lie (2014). His music was also used in the soundtrack for Ewan McGregor and Charlie Boorman's BBC series' Long Way Round and Long Way Down as well as NBC's short-lived action drama series, The Philanthropist.

Ayub has also acted under his birth name, Job Seda. He played Robert Redford's Maasai warrior assistant in Out of Africa (1985) and also starred in The Kitchen Toto (1987).

Ayub Ogada released the album Tanguru in 2007, the year Ayub moved back to Kenya.

In 2012, the English musician Trevor Warren went to Kenya to visit Ayub. Together with the Kenyan musician and engineer Isaac Gem, they composed and recorded the album Kodhi (meaning seed in Luo). Kodhi: Trevor Warren's Adventures with Ayub Ogada was released on Long Tale Recordings on 20 April 2015. Ayub was also included in the making of Queen Elizabeth II's diamond jubilee song which was played by the Commonwealth band with Gary Barlow under Andrew Lloyd Webber's direction. He is credited on the Kanye West album, Ye, as a co-songwriter of the track, "Yikes". He passed in February 2019.

Tanzania

Tanzania is located in Eastern Africa, bordering the Indian Ocean, between Kenya and Mozambique. The total area of Tanzania is 947,300sq km. The climate varies from tropical along coast to temperate in highlands. The main natural resources are hydropower, tin, phosphates, iron ore, coal, diamonds, gemstones, gold, natural gas, nickel.

The total population of Tanzania is 61,277,237 according to recent estimates. 2.81%

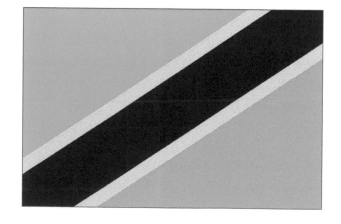

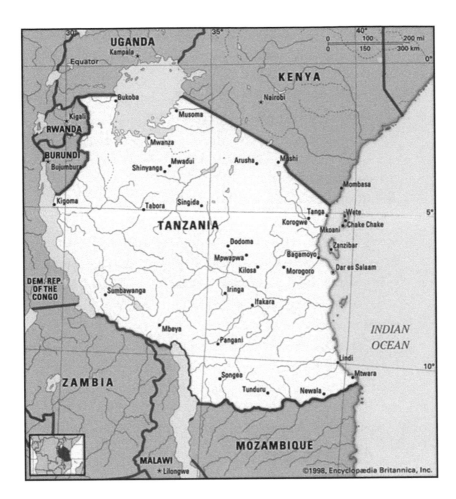

is the population growth rate. 36% of total population is urban population. Dar Es Salam (meaning Place of Peace) is its capital.

Mainland Tanzania fell under German rule during the late 19th century as part of German East Africa. After World War I, Britain governed the mainland as Tanganyika; the Zanzibar Archipelago remained a separate colonial jurisdiction. Tanzania became independent from Britain in the early 1960s, Tanganyika and Zanzibar merged to form the United Republic of Tanzania in 1964. The economy is based on agriculture and tourism which employs 65% of its workforce.

Ethnic Groups

The main ethnic group of Tanzanian Mainland are:

Africans constitute 99% of population. Of these 95% are Bantu consisting of more than 130 ethnic groups.

Other 1% consists of Asians, Europeans, and Arabs. For Zanzibar Archipelago ethnic groups include:

Africans, Arabs, Mixed Arab and African

These religious groups are prevalent in Tanzania:

Christian 61.4%, Muslim 35.2%, Folk religion 1.8%, Other 0.2%, Unaffiliated 1.4%

Languages

Kiswahili or Swahili are the official languages (Kiunguja is the name for Swahili in Zanzibar). English is also an official language and is the primary language of commerce, administration, and higher education. Arabic is manly spoken in Zanzibar. There are many local languages as well.

It is a constitutional republic with multi party representation.

Traditional Music

Music of Tanzania

The music of Tanzania is a microcosm of traditional African music using the string-based taarab linked to a distinctive Hip Hop rhythmic style known as bongo flava. The natural diversity of ethnic groups creates (120 ethnic groups living in Tanzania) a vast sonic landscape blending traditional musical and dance styles with corresponding instruments mixed with the contemporary influences of the modern world.

Taarab is a music genre popular in Tanzania and Kenya. It is influenced by the musical traditions of the African Great Lakes, North Africa, the Middle East, and the Indian subcontinent. Bongo Flava is one of the newest Tanzanian

genres, developed in the 1990s, and is a fusion genre. At its inception, Bongo flava was more heavily influenced by US Hip-Hop and Reggae, fused with traditional Tanzanian music styles. The current wind of nationalism among Tanzanian music consumers has begun favoring products from their local artists who sing in the national language, Swahili.

Contemporary artists like Diamond Platnumz, Juma Nature, Ali Kiba, Lady Jaydee and others have successfully reached a vast audience inside Tanzania, neighboring countries and abroad.

Hukwe Zawose

Hukwe Ubi Zawose was born in 1938 in the national capital of Tanzania, Dodoma. He was one of the most prominent Tanzanian musicians. He was a member of the Gogo ethnic group and played the ilimba, a large lamellophone similar to the mbira, as well as several other traditional instruments. He was also a highly regarded singer.

He came to national and international attention after President Julius Nyerere invited him to live and work in Dar es Salaam. He gained international attention for his cultural fusion work with Peter Gabriel, and released two albums (Chibite and Assembly) on Gabriel's Real World Records label. His final release before his death, Assembly, was a collaborative effort with producer/guitarist Michael Brook. At the 2005 Tanzania Music Awards he was given the Hall of Fame Award. His family is included in the 2009 documentary Throw Down Your Heart, which follows American banjo player Béla Fleck as he travelss through Africa. Hukwe Zawose was regarded as a cultural treasure in Tanzania due to its vast knowledge of Tanzanian traditional music and performance. He passed at the age of 63 on 30th December 2003.

Uganda

Uganda is located in East-Central Africa, west of Kenya, east of the Democratic Republic of the Congo. The total surface area of Uganda is 241,038 sq km. The climate is tropical; generally rainy with two dry seasons. The natural resources include copper, cobalt, hydropower, limestone, salt, arable land, and gold. The population of Uganda is 40.9 million. 24.4% of the total population of Uganda lives in urban areas. Its capital is Kampala.

British colonial rule and exploration began in the 1860s with explorers seeking the source of the Nile and expanded in subsequent decades with various trade agreements and the establishment of the Uganda Protectorate in 1894. As everywhere else in Africa, he colonial boundaries created by

Britain to delimit Uganda grouped together a wide range of ethnic groups with different political systems and cultures which made political progress and citizenship difficult. Independence was achieved in 1962.

Agriculture employs 72% of the work force. Key exports of Uganda are Coffee and Gold.

Ethnic Groups

The main ethnic groups of Uganda according to 2014 estimates are:

Baganda 16.5%, Banyankole 9.6%, Basoga 8.8%, Bakiga 7.1%, Iteso 7%, Langi 6.3%, Bagisu 4.9%, Acholi 4.4%, Lugbara 3.3%, other 32.1%

45.1% population of Uganda is Protestant. This includes:

Pentecostal/Born Again/Evangelical 11.1%, Seventh Day Adventist 1.7%, Baptist .3%, Anglican 32.0%

Whereas, 39.3% of population is Roman Catholic and 13.7% Muslim

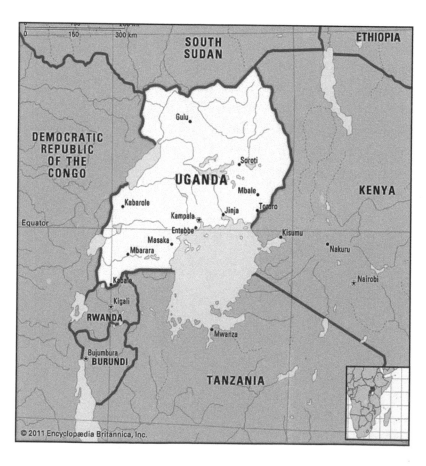

© 2011 Encyclopædia Britannica, Inc.

Languages

English is the official language. It is taught in schools, used in courts of law and by most newspapers and some radio broadcasts.

Ganda or Luganda are most widely used of the Niger-Congo languages and the language that is used most often in the capital. Other Niger-Congo languages include:

Nilo-Saharan languages, Swahili (official), Arabic. Uganda is a republic with multi party representation.

Uganda is a republic with multi party representation.

Contemporary Music

Samite Mulondo

Born in the early 50s, Samite is the stage name for East African musician Samite Mulondo. Originally from Uganda, Samite now lives in Tully, New York. He plays the flute and kalimba, a type of thumb piano.

A supremely gifted vocalist and a master of the kalimba, Samite likes to attribute his musical inspiration to both Ugandan folklore and as an expression of the life he experienced. He is very popular in Uganda and around the world. His music is a combination of native melodies and rhythms coupled with the organic sonic textures of the instrumentation found in the region of the Great Lakes. His unique musical melodic style ranges from danceable to meditative. Samite is also a co-founder of Musicians for World Harmony, a nonprofit organization that introduces music to African orphans. Samite co- founded the charity with his late wife, Joan. In 2005, Triloka Records released his 7th album Embalassa to rave reviews. He is one of the great ambassadors of African music worldwide.

Traditional Music of Uganda

Uganda is home to over 65 different ethnic groups. As such its traditional music is rich and diverse, textural and melodic. , Uganda forms the basis of all indigenous music. The Baganda ethnic group is responsible for much of the dissemination of the musical aesthetics in Unganda.

One of the early forms of popular music to grow out of traditional music was the Kadongo Kamu style. It was born out of traditional Kiganda musical expression. It became a dominant style of music in the 1980s. Artist Philly Lutaaya was responsible for much of its success.

In more contemporary times a new musical genre emerged in the 1990s entitled Afro Ragga locally called Kidandali. The artist Red Banton is recognized for generating much of the enthusiasm behind this more urban and contemporary style.

Mozambique

Mozambique is located in Southeastern Africa, bordering the Mozambique Channel, between South Africa and Tanzania. The total area of Mozambique is 799,380 sq km. Climate of Mozambique varies from tropical to subtropical. The main natural resources include coal, titanium, natural gas, hydropower, tantalum, and graphite.

The total population of Mozambique is 30.1 million, of which 37.1% is urban population. The capital of Mozambique is Maputo.

In the first half of the second millennium A.D., Northern Mozambican port towns were frequented by traders from Somalia, Ethiopia,

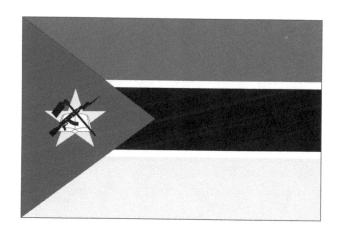

Egypt, Arabia, Persia, and India. The Portuguese were able to wrest much of the coastal trade from Arab Muslims in the centuries after 1500 and to set up their own colonies.

Portugal did not relinquish Mozambique until 1975 after a bloody battle with indigenous freedom fighters aided by Cuban Special Forces.

Ethnic Groups

The main ethnic groups in Mozambique are:

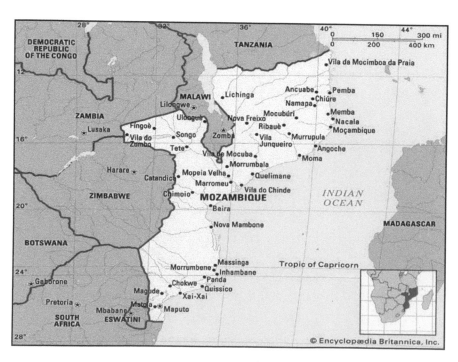

- 99% population is African. These ethnic groups include the Makhuwa, Tsonga, Lomwe, and Sena

- 0.8% population is Mestizo
- Other .2% include European, Indian, Pakistani, Chinese

The religions are;

- 27.2% is Roman Catholic, 18.9% is Muslim,
- 15.6% is Zionist Christian, 15.6% is Evangelical/Pentecostal
- Anglican 1.7%, Other 4.8%

Languages

Portuguese is the official language. Other languages include:

- Makhuwa 26.1%, Tsonga 8.6%, Nyanja 8.1, Sena 7.1%, Lomwe 7.1%, Chuwabo 4.7%, Ndau 3.8%, Tswa 3.8%
- Other Mozambican languages

Mozambique is a republic with multi party representation.

Traditional Music of Mozambique

In order to understand the music of Mozambique it is important to first realize that Mozambique like most African nations today, is a relatively new concept. Its borders were artificially created by the Portuguese crown present at the Berlin Conference of 1884 and lumped into a specific geographical area many, many different ethnic groups who historically had their own cultures, customs, traditions, therefore music. These different ethnic groups living in Mozambique such as the Makhuwa, Tsonga, Shona, Makonde, Sena, Ndau, and Chopi had their own specific cultural, melodic and rhythmic musical variations that define their aesthetic philosophies and identities before the term Mozambique was applied to their geographical area of existence.

The Portuguese arrive in the geographical area called Mozambique today in 1498 with explorer Vasco de Gama. They find an array of multicultural and multi religious communities composed of populations who have traded on the Swahili coast for centuries. Coexisting with the indigenous African

population were Arab communities, Chinese communities and populations of Indian descent. All of this to say that the concept of a Mozambican music is as new as its contemporary national existence, true of all independent nations of Africa with multiethnic representation.

Having said that the folk music of that region is colored by the use of its original African melodic and rhythmic cultures and textures, which existed before the ar-

▲ *Lupembe*

rival of the Portuguese. The use of the balafon like instruments called Mbila and the Mbira (thumb piano like instruments) along with various percussion instruments define the cultural identities of the African populations living in Mozambique. These musical instruments are usually handmade. Some of the instruments used in Mozambican musical expression include percussions made of wood and animal skin. The Lupembe is a woodwind instrument made from animal horns or wood.

At a first listen one would recognize the tropical quality, lilting rhythmic patterns and melodic inflections of Mozambican music and liken it to a form of island Calypso style. The reality is that by the time independence came in 1975, Mozambican bands began forging new musical forms of contemporary music forms based out of local folk styles fused with the new

African popular music coming from Zaire, Zimbabwe, Tanzania, and South Africa.

The Timbila style of music is an extremely intricate form of musical expression of the Chopi people who play the Mbila in an ensemble consisting of ten balafons of four different sizes with long compositional and complex musical structures that include an overture and ten different movements utilizing different tempos and rhythmic and melodic styles. The ensemble leader is responsible for simultaneously improvising a second contrapuntal line as he/she conducts the orchestra. When needed the concert master discusses with the dancers the adjustments that need to be made to bring the ceremony to a happy and culturally relevant conclusion.

The Marabenta style of music is urban in origin and a fusion of European styles and African influences and is the most popular danceable form of music in the country.

The Pandza style is by far the newest and most-popular style of Mozambican music. Its origin is credited to the artists N'Star, Ziqo and Dj Ardiles in Maputo. Pandza is especially popular amongst Mozambican youths and is a mix of Marrabenta and contemporary Pop.

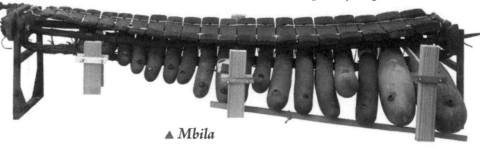

▲ *Mbila*

The roots of Pandza are in the Marrabenta style but Pandza has a faster tempo with major influences Hip Hop.

It is important to note that as influential Portugal was in that part of Africa, African culture similarly influenced and shaped the music of Brazil, Portugal's biggest colony in South America. African cultural influences can be heard in any and all popular musics of Brazil today as that country boasts the largest population of African descent outside of Africa, an estimated 97 million.

Contemporary Music of Mozambique

Fany Pfumo

Born in 1928, Fany Pfumo was one of the most influential early Marrabenta performers. He gained notoriety with his classic hit "Loko ni kumbuka Jorgina". His recordings made in South Africa for local labels later incorporated the South African Jazzy kwela music influences in his music. In 1979, he formed the Orchestra Marrabenta Star of Mozambique. The group travelled worldwide to great acclaim and he brought international recognition to the Marrabenta style. He passed in 1987.

Wazimbo

Humberto Carlos Benfica, aka Wazimbo was born November 11, 1948. He is considered one of the greatest voices of Mozambique and one of the most famous Marrabenta singers. Born in Chibuto he moved to the capital Maputo where he started as a vocalist for the "Silverstars" band. He later joined the Orchestra Marrabento Star de Mozambique with Fany Pfumo.

In 1972 he signed a contract as a professional singer and moved to Angola. After the independence, he sang with the big band of the national radio station, Radio Mocambique (RM). He became the lead vocalist of Orchestra Marrabenta Star de Moçambique in 1979. The Orchestra developed a full and funky style of Marrabenta music featuring electric guitars, powerful horn lines and soulful vocals under his leadership. Very successful at home in Mozambique, he toured Europe and released two CDs on Germany's Piranha record label with the band. Despite international acclaim the group called it quits in 1995. He is famous for his rendition of the ballad "Nwahulwana" ("night bird") released in 1988. The song was featured in a Microsoft commercial in California. In 2001 the song became part of the soundtrack for the movie The Pledge.

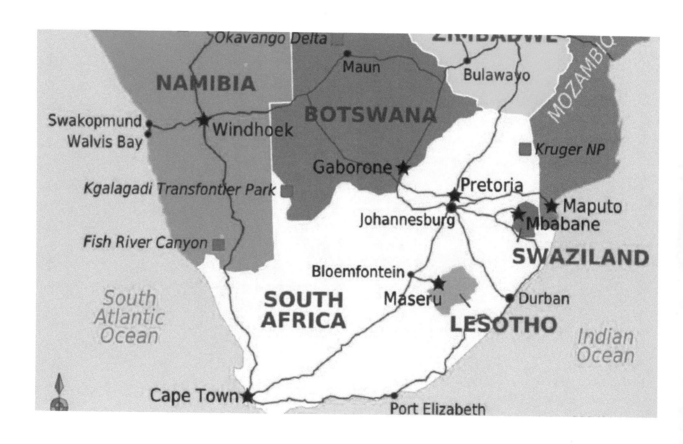

Chapter 8

South Africa; Namibia, Republic Of South Africa, Zimbabwe

Zimbabwe

Officially known as the Republic of Zimbabwe, the country is located in Southeast Africa between rivers Limpopo and Zambezi. The capital is Harare. Zimbabwe is bordered by South Africa, Botswana, Zambia, and Mozambique.

Zimbabwe has been known for multiple organized states and kingdoms since the start, and has been a major route for trade. After the British company rule of Cecil Rhodes ended at the turn of the 20th century the white minority government declared independence as Rhodesia from British rule. A fierce battle ensued between the indigenous Shona African populations supported by Cuban Special Forces and the Zimbabwe African National Union freedom fighters or ZANU organization led by commander and civil rights leader Robert Mugabe. The Shona people who represent the majority population of Zimbabwe won the military battles on the ground and forced the apartheid regime of Ian Smith out of the executive leadership of Rhodesia. A new name for the nation was given i.e. Zimbabwe and Robert Mugabe

became its first indigenous African president in 1980. The British government unhappy with Mugabe's management of the land redistribution process engaged in a worldwide economic embargo to defeat the Mugabe regime for two decades to no avail.

The country has seen major foreign exports in the form of minerals, gold, and agriculture. This has made the mining industry very lucrative. The country is home to some of the world's largest platinum reserves. It is not limited to platinum, Zimbabwe's Marange diamond fields are considered to be one of the biggest diamond finds over a century's time.

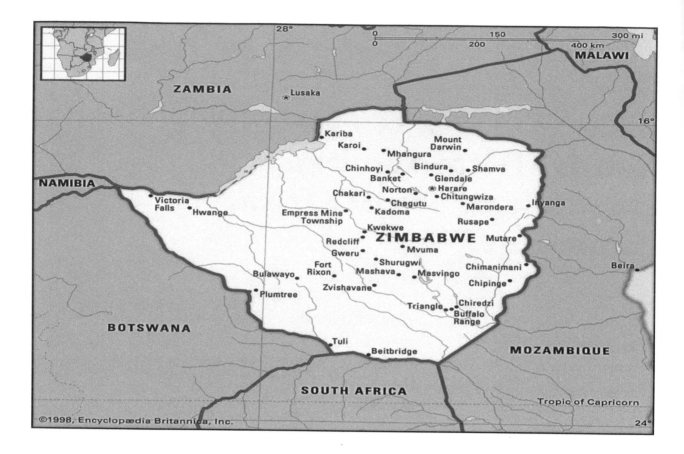

Ethnic Groups

Most of the population in the country is made up of 98% Bantu-speaking ethnic groups. Out of this, the majority is the Shona people, making 70%. The second most populous group is the Ndebele, making 20% of the population. Other ethnic groups include:

- ◆ Kalanga, Tonga, Shangaan, Venda, Sotho, Ndau, Nambya, Tswana, Xhosa, and Lozi. These groups make up 2-5% of the Bantu population.
- ◆ Other minority ethnic groups include white Zimbabweans, Afrikaner, Greek, Portuguese, French, Dutch and Indian and Asian communities.

Languages

There are 16 official languages in Zimbabwe, where English is the main language used in education and judicial systems.

- ◆ 70% of population speaks Shona, 20% Ndebele
- ◆ Minority Bantu languages include Venda, Tsonga, Shangaan, Kalanga, Sotho, Ndau, and Nambya.

Zimbabwe follows a presidential system of government. The House of Assembly is the lower chamber of the parliament. The upper chamber and the Senate were reinstated in 2005.

Contemporary Music of Zimbabwe

Oliver Tuku Mtukudzi

Born on the 22nd of September 1952, guitarist/vocalist Oliver Mtukudzi or Tuku was Zimbabwe's most renowned and internationally recognized musical and cultural icon. Leader of the band called the Black Spirits, Tuku's music was always danceable and socially and politically engaged. Due to his great popularity at home he began touring Europe and North America and developed a vast fan base on the world music circuit. He has appeared in several documentaries such as Under African Skies and The Soul of Mbira, produced by BBC. Tuku passed on the 23rd of January 2019, in Harare, Zimbabwe. He leaves an enormous legacy of music and socially conscious texts that continue to inspire and energize the next generation of artists worldwide.

Thomas Mapfumo

Nicknamed 'The Lion of Zimbabwe' and 'Mukanya', Thomas Tafirenyika Mapfumo was born on the 3rd of July, 1945 in Marondera. Mapfumo is the reason Chimurenga music exists and is popular.

Mapfumo joined the Zutu Brothers as a singer at the age of 16. For many years he went from one band to another. For many years he performed American rock cover songs and soul music. He began adapting Shona traditional music to modern instrumentation. Mapfumo also did farming and raised chickens. His 1972 band was named the Hallelujah Chicken Run Band. Politically engaged he was sent to prison by the Rhodesian government threw and was released thanks to public pressure. Thomas Mapfumo continues to tour internationally and sings about the struggles of the people of Zimbabwe. His musical style is called the Chimurenga style.

Traditional Music of Zimbabwe

Music of Mbira

Music has always been an important part of the Zimbabwean society and culture with the music being heavily reliant on different instruments such as the mbira. This family of musical instruments are traditional to Shona people of Zimbabwe. The Mbira became popular in the 1960s and early

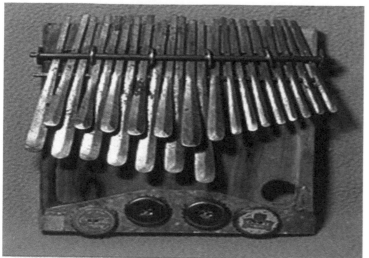

medication and relaxation. This instrument is played seen and heard throughout the Swahili coast and deep in the countryside. It comes in varied configurations.

Mbira consists of tines, and these were originally made of bamboo but during the passage of time, almost 1,300 years ago, metal keys were developed to create a fine tuned sound. In the entire history of idiophones and lamellaphones, Mbira like instruments appeared almost 3,000 years ago (Kubik, 1998).

1970s and was also known as Kalimba. Musicians used Mbira along with modern rock instruments with the likes of electric guitar and bass, horns, and drum kits. Its soft textural colors and soothing tonalities make him a perfect instrument for

There are many variations of Mbira, with thousands of different tunings, designs, and note layouts but there is a specific tuning and note style of the original metal tined instrument which is dated back to 1,300 years ago, and that is known as the 'Kalimba core'.

Namibia

Namibia is a country in southern Africa, bordered to the west by the Atlantic Ocean, Angola and Zambia to the north, Botswana to the east, and lastly, South Africa to the south-east. Its capital city is Windhoek. The country's total surface area is 825,615 sq. km, sparsely populated by only 2.55 million people. It is the driest country—with the least rainfall—in sub-Saharan Africa, and has an arid climate which includes more than 300 days of sunshine per year.

Manufacturing is the nation's largest economic sector, constituting 13.5% of the total GDP, followed by mining at 10.4% and agriculture at 5.0%. The banking sector has also been highly developed with such modern infrastructure as mobile and internet banking. Namibia is the fourth largest producer of uranium in the world and a primary source of gem-quality

diamonds. The country also exports copper, fluorspar, gold, lead, manganese, marble, tin, tungsten, and zinc.

Namibia became independent on the 21st of March 1990, after the Namibian War of Independence led by the freedom fighters of the South West African People's Organization

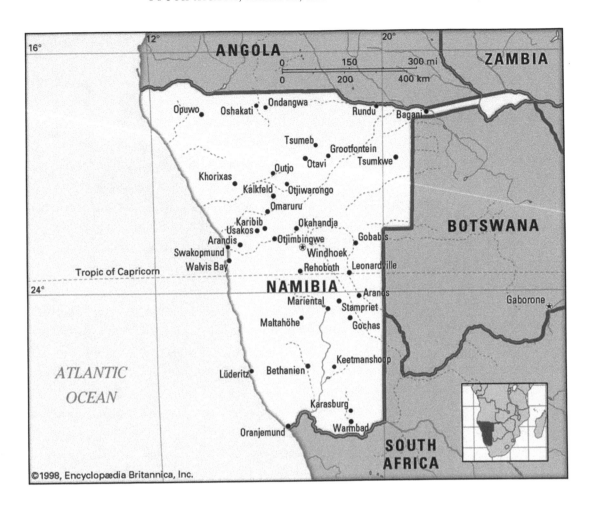

(SWAPO) trained and supported by the Cuban Special Forces. SWAPO finally ended the mind numbing agreement put together by the United Nations which had allowed the South African Apartheid Government to control the territory of Namibia taken away from colonial Germany at the end of World War II.

14 regions altogether make up the entire country of Namibia, and these regions are further divided into 121 constituencies. Keeping foreign relations in check, Namibia is part of the United Nations (UN), the Southern African Development Community (SADC), the African Union (AU), and the Commonwealth of Nations.

Ethnic Groups

The main ethnic groups of Namibia:

◆ Majority is of Ovambo ethnicity, Bantu speaking origin
◆ Similar language group includes Herero and Himba people, and another similar speaking language group includes Nama and Damara
◆ Minor ethnic groups include refugees from Angola, Chinese
◆ Smaller groups with mixed racial origins called 'Coloureds' and 'Basters' that make up 8% of the population

Whites – German, Portuguese, British, and Afrikaner make up around 4% to 7% of the population

Languages

English is considered as the official language of Namibia. Other includes:

◈ Oshiwambo (49%), Khoekhoegowab (11.3%), Afrikaans (10.4%), RuKwangali (9%), SiLozi (4.8), Otjiherero (9%), and other African languages (1.2%).

Namibia is a unitary semi-presidential representative democratic republic.

Contemporary Music of Namibia

From the 1960s to 1990s, Political music was very popular in Namibia. This genre mostly contained songs that reflected peace, love, war, family, and friendship. Post 2000s, Kwaito music is the most popular genre in Namibia, having the most amount of artists and fans.

Other genres include hip hop, R&B, Soul, Reggae, house, and afro-pop. Rhythm and Blues turn-producer Big Ben is one of the most respected artist because of his Afro pop style music, performing everywhere with a live band.

Music is slowly changing in the country, with genres mixing together to make new trendy music. The White communities in Namibia closely celebrate Rock n Roll, with Die Vogel being the country's most exceptional band in this music genre.

Like Western counter parts, Hip Hop genre is also especially popular with the youth of Namibia. This type of music is mostly inspired by the American Hip Hop culture, particularly rappers like Eminem, Jay Z, Snoop Dogg, and the likes of such. Even though that is the case, some Namibian artists prefer to sing in their own language, staying true to their culture.

Traditional Music of Namibia

Namibia has retained its traditional music scene. Communal music is practiced mostly in the Northern areas of the country. This includes music related to specific functions which can be daily or seasonal. Traditional music varies according to cultural differences.

The most common type of traditional Namibian music is Folk music. Folk music consists of multiple music types like Oviritje, Malgaisa, Shambo, and Afrikaans.

Shambo is traditionally considered the dance music of Oshiwambo – speaking people, deriving its name from Shambo Shakambode. Malgaisa is another dance music genre which is also known as Damara Punch. This genre is performed by Damara Dikding, Stanley, Aubasen, and Dixson. Afrikaans is influenced by European folk music and is mostly popular with white communities in Namibia.

Even though these genres are different, they are being mixed under the emblem of Folk music, highlighting the traditional music of Namibia. By mixing these together, unique songs are made that enables Namibian artists to tap into unique vocal sets and create distinguishing music.

Republic of South Africa

With over 60 million people, Republic of South Africa (RSA) is the southernmost country in entire Africa. The RSA is also one of the largest countries in the world, being the world's 23rd most populous nation. The country has three capital cities; Pretoria, Bloemfontein, and Cape Town.

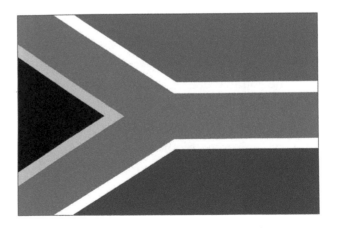

Covering 1,221,037 sq. km, the country is surrounded by the coastline along the Indian Oceans and South Atlantic. Being this big, the country is extremely diverse with different species of animals as well as plants. RSA is known to have over 200,000 fungi species, excluding fungi associated with insects.

Convention on Biological Diversity was signed by South Africa in 1994 and the country became a party to the convention in 1995. Being ranked as sixth out of the world's seventeen most mega-diverse country, it has produced a National Biodiversity Strategy and Action Plan.

Tourism has been on the rise in South Africa, with most of the country's revenue coming through the tourism industry. Apart from earning

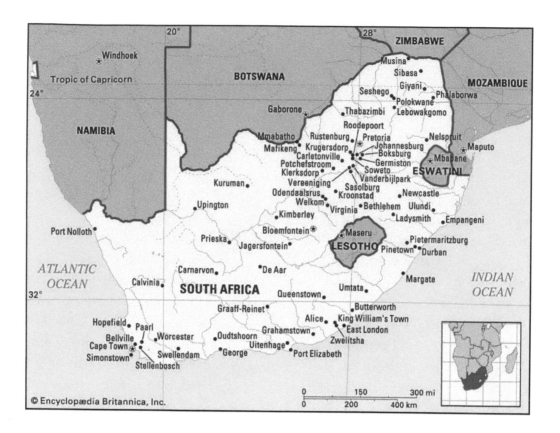

revenue through tourism, RSA is considered to be a powerhouse for mining, especially of minerals, gold, and diamond. With abundance of minerals and precious metals, the country is the largest producer of Manganese, Platinum, Vanadium, Chrome, and Vermiculite.

The country does not have a legally defined capital city. RSA, being the Union of South Africa, was the founding member of the UN. The country is also one of the founding members of the African Union (AU), having the third largest economy among the members.

Ethnic Groups

The ethnic groups in South Africa include:

- Black South Africans (78.4%)
- White South African (10.2%)
- Colored South Africans (8.8%)
- Indian South African/Asians (2.6%)
- Other/unspecified (0.5%)

Apart from these, there are small groups of Chinese, Pakistanis, Vietnamese, Nigerians, Somalis, and Zimbabweans

Languages

There are 11 official languages in South Africa. These include:

Zulu (22.7%), Xhosa (16%), Afrikaans (13.5%), English (9.6%), Pedi (9.1%), Tswana (8%), Southern Sotho (7.6%), Tsonga (4.5%), Swazi (2.5%), Venda (2.4%), Southern Ndebele (2.1%)

RSA is a parliamentary republic. Each of the nine provinces are governed by a unicameral legislature, which is elected every five years by party-list proportional representation

Contemporary Music of South Africa

Hugh Masekela

Hugh Ramapolo Masekela, born in 1939, is known as the Father of South African Jazz. Being a South African trumpeter, cornetist, flugelhornist, singer, and a composer, made a number of jazz compositions. He is known for writing well-recognized anti-apartheid songs, the likes of which includes Bring Him Back Home and Soweto Blues. A great composer and Jazz trumpet master Hugh Masekela compositional style opened the way forward for young African composers in the musical fusion of styles of the African diaspora.

He is an immensely important composer of Black music who brought the vocabulary of improvisation of Charlie Parker and Dizzy Gillespie in the world of continental African musical languages.

To spread political change, he made music portraying the struggles and sorrows of the country alongside joys and passions. In 1958, after the Manhattan Brothers tour of South Africa, Masekela joined the orchestra of the musical King Kong. Hugh, along with other artists formed the Jazz Epistles, which was the first African jazz group, recording an LF. Moving to the United States after securing a scholarship back in London, Masekela studied classical trumpet from 1960 to 1964 at Manhattan School of Music in New York. His hits in the US include Up, Up and Away and Grazing in the Grass, the latter becoming the number- one smash, selling over four million copies.

Masekela passed in Johannesburg, South Africa on 23rd January 2018.

Miriam Makeba

Zenzile Miriam Makeba aka Mama Africa, was a songwriter, singer, and actress but also a United Nations' goodwill ambassador and civil rights activist. She was born in Johannesburg on 4th March, 1932. Working in different genres like Jazz, Afropop, and world music, she became an advocate against apartheid in her own country. She was subsequently sent in exile by the Apartheid government of South Africa.

Getting a brief role in anti-apartheid film Come Back, Africa, she garnered international attention which led her to perform in London, New York, and Venice. She moved to New York City which proved to be quite successful as she

Miriam Makeba

became popular immediately. Makeba recorded her first solo album in 1960. From there on, her career prospered in the United States, where she released numerous songs and albums along her most popular song Pata Pata. She joined the cause of African Americans and the Black Panther movement battling Jim Crow laws in the United States. There, she received support from the Caribbean superstar vocalist and actor Harry Belafonte. Miriam Makeba was the voice of Africa abroad and her steadfast advocacy against Apartheid South Africa gave her moral authority. In 1965, she earned a Grammy Award for her album An Evening with Belafonte/Makeba. She appeared in the film Sarafina! In 1992. After becoming the goodwill ambassador for the UN, she campaigned for several humanitarian causes. Miriam Makeba passed in Castel Volturno, Italy, on 9th November 2008.

Abdullah Ibrahim

Born as Adolph Johannes Brand on October 1934, and being known as Dollar Brand earlier, Abdullah Ibrahim is a pianist and composer. The inspiration and influence in his music comes from his childhood in port areas of Cape Town that were culturally diverse. Discovered by none of Duke Ellington in Switzerland he will move to New York City and becomes a fixture of the Jazz scene. His weekly concerts at the famed Sweet Basil of New York are legendary. His music encompasses traditional

South African melodic and rhythmic traditions but also South African gospel music, and modern Jazz. Abdullah Ibrahim is also considered to be one of the leading figures in the subgenre of Cape Jazz. He is the first African to receive the United States National Endowment for the Arts Jazz Distinction, the NEA Jazz Master Award.

In the anti-apartheid anthems, his jazz composition "Mannenberg" is a standout. Abdullah Ibrahim has been a headliner at countless Jazz festivals worldwide.

Sharon Katz

Born in Port Elizabeth, South Africa in the 1960s, she is a South African vocalist, guitarist, composer and music therapist who joined the ANC movement against the Apartheid regime of South Africa as a teenager. After Graduate music studies in the United States she returned home to South Africa and created the 500 voices multiracial, multicultural youth choir and toured South Africa in a train called the "Peace Train". Heralded by President Nelson Mandela as one of the great South Africans, her 2015 documentary film "When Voices Meet" showcasing her

500 multiracial children choir in South Africa received awards worldwide. She continues to be active with the Peace Train and civil rights issues at home and abroad.

Ladysmith Black Mambazo

Ladysmith Black Mambazo is a South African male choral group singing in the South African tradition of vocal style and heritage called isicathamiya and

mbube. American superstar guitarist/ vocalist Paul Simon discovered them in South Africa and asked them to participate in the recording of his 1986 album entitled Graceland. The immediate success of Graceland brought Ladysmith Black Mambazo international recognition and they began touring

worldwide. Recipients of 5 Grammy awards they continue to be South Africa's best musical and cultural ambassadors. The iconic band was formed by vocal leader Joseph Shabalala in 1960.

Traditional Music of South Africa
Music of Zulu

Zulu music comes from the Zulu people who are a South African ethnic group. The entire South African music consists of a major part of Zulu musicians through which, music styles that are derived from Zulu-folk have gained recognition across South Africa as well as abroad. The genres that make up Zulu music includes Kwaito, Maskandi, Kasi Rap, Rawkat, Gqomu, Mbube and Isicathamiya, and Modern Zulu.

Similar to Electronic and Hip Hop music, the Kwaito genre is a form of house music which highlights African sounds and samples. Maskandi, on the other hand, is evolving with more women making music in this genre. Kasi Rap genre, originating from Emzansi, accommodates a lot of rappers.

Featuring different bass and wavy beats, Gqomu emerged from the city of Durban and has gained popularity in LondoMbube and Isicathamiya is South African music that became a hit in Swaziland. Modern Zulu consists of different styles, produced through a mix of rock and Zulu folk music.

Chapter 9

Central Africa; Cameroon, Congo, Angola

Country of CameroonCameroon is a country lying at the junction of western and central Africa. Its ethnically diverse population is among the most urban in western Africa. The capital is Yaoundé, located in the south-central part of the country. The country's name is from Rio dos Camarões, literally translating to "River of Prawns." Until the late 19th century, English usage confined the term

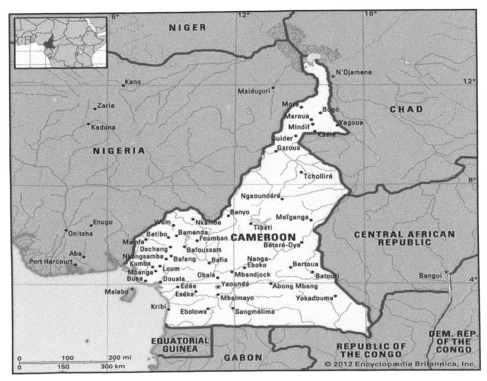

Central Africa

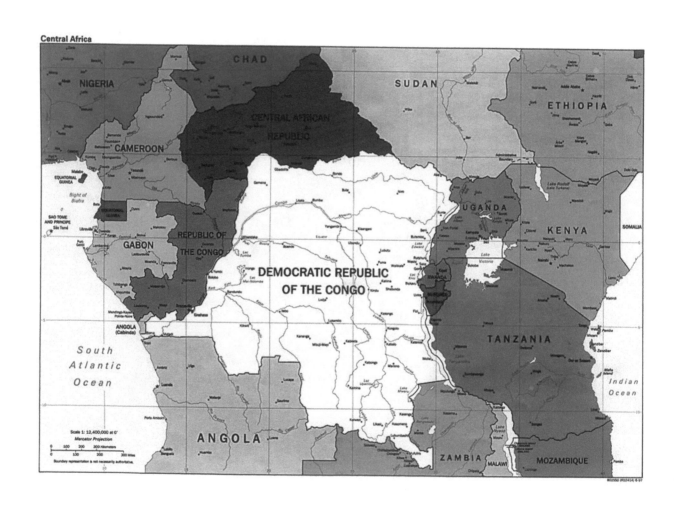

"the Cameroons" to the mountains, while the estuary was called the Cameroons River.

Present-day Cameroon was first settled in the Neolithic Era. The longest continuous inhabitants are groups such as the Baka (Pygmies). From there, Bantu migrations into eastern, southern, and central Africa are believed to have occurred about 2,000 years ago. The Sao culture arose around Lake Chad, c. 500 AD, and gave way to the Kanem and its successor state, the Bornu Empire. Kingdoms, fandoms, and chiefdoms arose in the west.

Cameroon's legal system is a mixture of civil law, common law, and customary law. Although nominally independent, the judiciary falls under the authority of the executive's Ministry of Justice. The president appoints judges at all levels. The judiciary is officially divided into tribunals, the court of appeal, and the Supreme Court. The National Assembly elects the members of a nine-member High Court of Justice that judges high-ranking government members if they are charged with high treason or harming national security.

The population of Cameroon was 25,216,267 in 2018. The life expectancy was 62.3 years – 60.6 years for males and 64 years for females. Both English and French are official languages, although French is by far the most understood language, i.e., more than 80%. Cameroon has a high level of religious freedom and diversity. The predominant faith is Christianity, practiced by about two-thirds of the population, while Islam is a significant minority faith, adhered to by about one-fourth. Muslims are most concentrated in the north, while Christians are concentrated primarily in the southern and western regions.

Contemporary Music

The earliest recorded popular music from Cameroon comes from the 1930s, when the most popular styles were imported pop music and French-style chanson. In Douala, the most developed city in Cameroon, accordions and ambasse bey music were common, with performers like Lobe Lobe, Ebanda Manfred, and Nelle Eyoum finding a local audience. Ekambi Brillant and the first major Cameroonian hit, "N'Gon Abo," set the stage for the development of makossa. Post-independence in 1960, a local variant on palm wine music called assiko, was popular especially Jean Bikoko and Dikoume Bernard.

The urbanization of Cameroon has had a major influence on the country's music. Migration to the city of Yaoundé, for example, was a major cause for the popularization of bikutsi music. During the 1950s, bars sprang up across the city to accommodate the influx of new inhabitants and soon became a symbol for

Cameroonian identity in the face of colonialism. Balafon orchestras, consisting of 3-5 balafons and various percussion instruments (including the balafon, which is both a harmonic and percussive instrument) became common in the bars. Some of these orchestras, such as Richard Band de Zoetele, became quite popular in spite of scorn from the European elite.

Hence, the music of Cameroon includes diverse traditional and modern musical genres. The best-known contemporary genre is makossa, a popular style that has gained fans across Africa, and its related dance craze bikutsi. The pirogue sailors of Douala are known for a kind of singing called ngoso, which has evolved into a kind of modern music accompanied by zanza, balafon, and various percussion instruments.

Manu Dibango

Emmanuel N'Djoké born on 12th December 1933. He is best known by his stage name Manu Dibango. He is considered in Africa as the Dean of African modern music. Originally, from Cameroon, he is a composer, saxophonist and xylophonist of great importance. He developed an African musical style fusing jazz, funk, and traditional Cameroonian rhythms and melodic systems showing the way to future African composers. He is remembered as the first African musician to make it on the American Billboard with his 1972 single "Soul Makossa". Manu Dibango collaborated with a myriad of musicians, including Fania All Stars, Fela Kuti, Herbie Hancock, Bill Laswell, Bernie Worrell, Ladysmith Black Mambazo, King Sunny Adé, Don Cherry, and Sly and Robbie. He achieved a considerable following in the UK with a disco hit called "Big Blow", originally re-leased in 1976 and re-mixed as a 12″ single in 1978 on Island Records. In 1998, he recorded the album CubAfrica with Cuban artist Eliades Ochoa. At the 16th Annual Grammy Awards in 1974, he was nominated in the categories for Best R&B Instrumental Performance and Best Instrumental Composition for "Soul Makossa". Manu Dibango passed on March 24, 2020.

Francis Bebey

Francis Bebey born on 15th July 1929 in Douala, Cameroon was a Cameroonian writer and composer. In the early 1960s, Bebey moved to France and started work in the arts, establishing himself as a musician, sculptor, and writer. His most popular novel was Agatha Moudio's Son. While working at UNESCO from 1961-74, he became the head of the music department in Paris. This job allowed him to research and document traditional African music.

Bebey released his first album in 1969. His music was primarily guitar-based, but he integrated traditional African instruments and synthesizers as well. Though Bebey is currently praised for his music, his musical taste created controversy with his native mu-sic when he first started off. His style merged Cameroonian makossa with classical guitar, jazz, and pop and was considered by critics to be groundbreaking, intellectual, humorous, and profoundly sensual.

He sang in Duala, English, and French. Bebey helped launch the career of Manu Dibango. Bebey released more than 20 albums over his career. He passed in Paris, France, on 28 May 2001 leaving an exceptional legacy behind. His sur-vivors include his children Patrick, Toups, and Kidi Bebey, and his wife.

John Williams' piece "Hello Francis" is written as a tribute to Bebey: "The piece is based on the Makossa, a popular dance rhythm from Cameroon often used by Francis, and includes a quote from his piece The Magic Box and a hid-den bit of J.S. Bach." Arcade Fire's song, "Everything Now," features a flute part from "The Coffee Cola Song" by Francis Bebey. The flute part was played by Patrick Bebey, Francis Bebey's son.

Traditional Music

The ethnicities of Cameroon include an estimated 250 distinct ethnic groups in five regional-cultural divisions. An estimated 38% of the population are Western highlanders–Semi-Bantu or grass fielders, including the Bamileke, Bamum, and many smaller Tikar groups in the northwest. 12% are coastal tropical forest peoples, including the Bassa, Duala, and many smaller groups in the southwest.

The southern tropical forest peoples (18%) include the Beti-Pahuin and their sub-groups, the Bulu and Fang, the Maka and Njem, and the Baka pygmies. In the semi-arid northern regions (the Sahel) and central highlands, the Fulani (French: Peul or Peuhl; Fula: Fulɓe) form an estimated 14% of Cameroonians, while the Kirdi (unbelievers) are a general category, comprising 18% of the population, of various mainly Chadic and Adamawa speakers.

BaAka People of Cameroon & their music

The BaAka people inhabit the rain forests of Cameroon, the Republic of the Congo, the Central African Republic, and Gabon. Outcast from neighboring societies due to their short stature and nomadic lifestyle, the BaAka have retained their own language and ancient forms of cultural expression. BaAka music is similar to other pygmy ethnic groups' music around Africa, signified by polyphonic vocal choirs, with several melodies sung simultaneously and polyrhythmic percussion.

The "singing the song" is done by the women, while the men "march the song" (dance). The only musical accompaniment is percussion consisting of simple drums, rattles, and iron blades struck against each other. This mid-1970s recording was made by Simha Arom and Phillipe Renaud. Arom, a noted expert on the music of central Africa, also co-wrote the liner notes. In addition to this album, Arom's recordings are featured on more than a dozen other albums in the UNESCO Collection of Traditional Music, including Musical Sources and Symphony of Nature.

Musical Instruments of Cameroon

▲ *Bamileke drummers*

◀ *Slit gong*

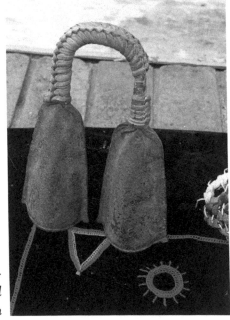

Vessel rattles ▶
made of wood
in Cameroon

Country of Congo

The Democratic Republic of the Congo, also known as Congo-Kinshasa, DR Congo, the DRC, the DROC, or simply either Congo or the Congo, and formerly Zaire, is a country in Central Africa. It is, by area, the largest country in sub-Saharan Africa, the second-largest in all of Africa, and the 11th-largest in the world.

With a population of around 105 million, the Democratic Republic of the Congo is the most populous officially Francophone country in the world, as well as the fourth-most populous country in Africa and the 15th-most populous country in the world. It is a member of the United Nations, Non-Aligned Movement, African Union, and COMESA. Since 2015, the Eastern DR Congo

has been the site of an ongoing military conflict in Kivu. The capital and largest city are Kinshasa.

Centered on the Congo Basin, the territory of the DRC was first inhabited by Central African foragers around 90,000 years ago and was reached by the Bantu expansion about 3,000 years ago. In the west, the Kingdom of Kongo ruled around the mouth of the Congo River from the 14th to 19th centuries. In the northeast, center, and east, the kingdoms of Azande, Luba, and Lunda ruled from the 16th and 17th centuries to the 19th century.

In the 1870s, just before the onset of the Scramble for Africa, European exploration of the Congo Basin was carried out, first led by

Henry Morton Stanley under the sponsorship of Leopold II of Belgium. Leopold formally acquired rights to the Congo territory at the Berlin Conference in 1885 and declared the land his private property, naming it the Congo Free State.

During the Free State, his colonial military unit, the Force Publique, forced the local population to produce rubber. From 1885 to 1908, millions of Congolese people died as a consequence of disease and exploitation. In 1908, despite his initial reluctance, Leopold ceded the so-called Free State to Belgium; thus, it became known as the Belgian Congo. The shameful and criminal treatment by the Belgians of the indigenous Bantu populations working on rubber plantations was revealed to the world in the 1980s and drew worldwide condemnation. Congo achieved its independence from Belgium June 30th, 1960 under the name Republic of the Congo. A confluence of deplorable events involving the Belgians, the United Nations and various other western interests resulted in the removal

and subsequent assassination of Congo's first democratically elected prime minister Patrice Lumumba in 1961. The subsequent installation of Mobutu Sese Seko by western nations and their funded mercenaries will create a guerilla war that will last more than 30 years thus ravaging the economy of a nation which is immensely rich. The Cuban government was asked by the opposition to Mobutu to intervene and it sent its Special Forces as trainers and support teams as well as importing its soft power i.e. education of physicians, engineers, teachers, military personnel and of course musicians, hence its cultural influence....

Contemporary Music:

While it is true that Bantu traditional music made its way to the island of Cuba via the Atlantic Slave trade of the Spanish era, the contemporary music of the DRC takes its influence from the contemporary Cuban music named rumba. That Cuban influence will give birth to a new indigenous

musical style called Soukous. Other African nations will draw musical inspiration from Soukous to produce other related musical genres in Kenya, Tanzania, Uganda etc...no one epitomized this musical style more than the Congolese guitarist/vocalist Franco and its archrival Papa Wemba.

Franco

Franco Luambo Makiadi will forever remain in the collective memory of the Congolese as the undisputed "King of Rumba." Born July 6th, 1938, in the Democratic Republic of the Congo, he is most commonly referred to like Franco, he was nicknamed the "Sorcerer of the Guitar," as he mastered the skills of playing fluidly with seemingly little effort. During a span of 40 years in the music industry, Franco produced over 100 albums and approximately 1,000 songs to his name.

Through the 1960s, Franco and O.K. Jazz toured regularly and recorded prolifically. By 1967 Franco was a co-leader of the band, with vocalist Vicky. When Vicky left in 1970, Franco became the sole leader of the band. And then, another change to Tout Puissant O.K. Jazz (T.P.O.K. Jazz) (which stands in French for The Almighty O.K. Jazz)

In 1978, Franco was imprisoned for two months by Zaire's President Mobutu for the lyrics to his songs Helene and Jackie. Later the same year, however, President Mobutu decorated him for his musical contributions.

Franco played in the United States once, in 1983, appearing twice in New York's Manhattan Center. In his thirty-three years with the band, Franco and TPOK Jazz released hundreds of singles and over 100 albums. His music blended Cuban rumba with local Congolese rhythms, attracting both the young and the elderly. His influence can be heard in local music today and remains popular in nightclubs.

Franco passed October 12, 1989, at Namur in Belgium.

Papa Wemba

Papa Wemba is such an important figure in Congolese music that it is nearly impossible to compete. Born on 14 June 1949, he was dubbed the "King of Rumba Rock" and was one of the most popular musicians of his time in Africa and played an important role in world music. He was also a fashion icon who popularized the Sape look and style through his musical group Viva la Musica, with whom he performed on stages throughout the world.

Papa Wemba's road to fame and prominence began when he joined the music group Zaiko Langa Langa in the late 1960s. This was followed by his success as a founding member both of Isifi Lokole and then Yoka Lokole, along with a short stint as a member of Afrisa International for a few months. During these early stages of his career, he was establishing a style that included traditional Congolese rumba and soukous, infused with traditional African sounds, Caribbean rhythms, rock and soul. But Wemba gained international success and status with his band Viva La Musica, especially after he took them to Paris, France in the early 1980s. It was there that Wemba was able to achieve more of an "eclectic sound" in his work, influenced by western popular music that reflected a European flavor and style, referred to as Europop.

Papa Wemba

Hence, regardless of the popular hits and artists, the first name that comes to mind when thinking about Congolese music and rumba is Papa Wemba. With songs such as "Analengo," Papa Wemba is not only one of the most popular artists in Africa but also a prominent figure in world music.

Wemba passed at the age of 66 in Abidjan, Côte d'Ivoire, during the FEMUA urban music festival on Sunday, 24 April 2016.

Pepe Kalle

Pépé Kallé, sometimes written as Pepe Kalle was a soukous singer, musician and bandleader from Congo. Pépé Kallé was born on November 30, 1951 in Kabasele Yampanya in Kinshasa (then Léopoldville) in the Belgian Congo. However, he later assumed his pseudonym in hommage to his mentor, Le Grand Kallé. With a multi-octave vocal reach and a unique stage presence, the 190 cm (6ft 3in) and 136 kg (300lb) entertainer recorded multiple hundred melodies and twenty collections during his two-very long term profession. He was referred to warmly as "the elephant of African music" and "La Bombe Atomique," Kallé engaged crowds with his hearty exhibitions.

His melodic profession began with l'African Jazz, the band of Le Grand Kallé. He later acted in Bella and turned into the lead artist of Lipua, where he sang close by Nyboma Mwandido. In 1972, Kallé, alongside Dilu Dilumona and Papy Tex, passed on Lipua to shape their band named Empire Bakuba. Realm Bakuba took its name from a Congolese champion clan, and it distinctly fused rootsy rhythms from the inside, sounds that had for quite some time been sidelined by famous rumba. The band was a moment hit, and along with Zaiko Langa, they turned into Kinshasa's most well-known youth band. With hits, for example, Pépé Kallé's Dadou and Papy Tex's Sango ya mawa, the band was a consistent installation on the graphs. They likewise made another dance, the kwassa kwassa.

On November 28, 1998, Pépé Kallé suffered a heart attack at his home in Kinshasa and was rushed to the nearby Clinique Ngaliema. Shortly after midnight on Sunday November 29, Pépé Kallé passed.

Country of Angola

Angola, officially the Republic of Angola, is a country on the west coast of Southern Africa. It is the second-largest Lusophone (Portuguese-speaking) country in both total area and population (behind Brazil) and is the seventh-largest country in Africa. Namibia borders it to the south, DR Congo to the north, Zambia to the east, and the Atlantic Ocean to the west. Angola has an exclave province, the province of Cabinda, which borders the Republic of the Congo and the Democratic Republic of the Congo. The capital and the most populated city is Luanda.

Angola has been inhabited since the Paleolithic Age. Its formation as a nation-state originates from Portuguese colonization, which initially began with coastal settlements and trading posts founded in the 16th century. In the 19th century, European settlers gradually began to establish themselves in the interior. The Portuguese colony that became Angola did not have its present borders until the early 20th century, owing to resistance by native groups such as the Cuamato, the Kwanyama, and the Mbunda.

During the late 1950s, the rise of the Marxist–Leninist Popular Movement for the Liberation of Angola (MPLA) in the east and Dembos hills north of Luanda came to hold special significance. In addition to the MPLA two other parties contributed to the independence movement and its independence from Portugal in 1975. After a long protracted struggle against mercenaries financed by Western nations and the United States on behalf of the FNLA and UNITA, Angola through the MPLA with the help of a massive amount of Cuban Special Forces won the decisive battles at Cuito Carnavale in the late 1980s.

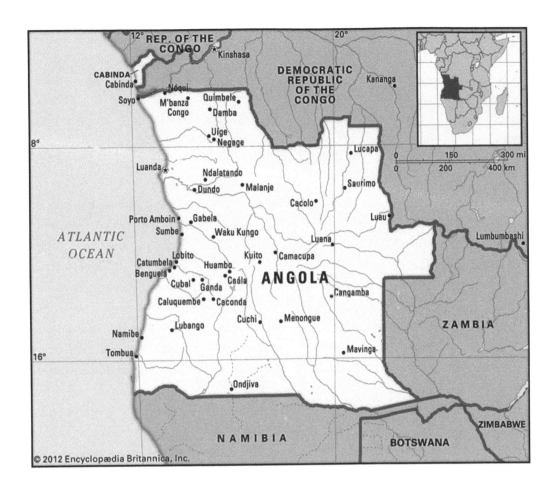

© 2012 Encyclopædia Britannica, Inc.

Contemporary Music Section

From wider musical trends to political history of the country – various reasons have shaped the music of Angola for the better. The capital and biggest city of Angola, Luanda, is home to various styles, including kilapanda, semba, kizomba, and kuduro. Simply off the shore of Luanda is Ilha do Cabo, home to an accordion and harmonica-based style of music called rebita.

Angola's famous music has had minimal global achievement. During the 1800s, Angolan performers in the urban areas tried different things with well-known styles worldwide, including dances and anthems. With the primary portion of the 20th century came huge groups, who sang in Portuguese and Kimbundu.

The main gathering to be known outside of Angola was Duo Ouro Negro, made in 1956. After a fruitful sting in Portugal, the pair visited Switzerland, France, Finland, Sweden, Denmark, and Spain.

After they came, Orquestra os Jovens do Prenda, who were generally famous from the last part of the 1960s to the mid-1970s, proceeded to perform and record inconsistently. The huge band included two trumpets, a saxophone, four guitars, and six percussion instruments. They played kizomba (a local style based around the marimba xylophone), utilizing the four guitars to estimate the marimba and quilapanga.

Other than the mid-60s until the late 70s, a few different gatherings like Kiezos, Negoleiros

both during the period of Portuguese colonization and after independence.

Two other unmistakable artists of the pre-autonomy period included David Zé and Urbano de Castro, both of whom were killed because of their political activism.

Starting during the 1970s, Bonga turned into the most notable Angolan pop performer outside the country. Born in 1942 Jose Adelino Barcelo de Carvalho aka Bonga Kwenda (name of artist), he started acting in the mid-1960s when Angolan people's music discovered some prominence. As an individual from Kissueia, he resolved social issues while turning into a soccer star. He was moved to Lisbon by the pilgrim government, and he there played soccer until 1972, when he left to fight Portugal's frontier battle in Angola. Bonga's "Mona Ki Ngi Xica" (1972) acquired him a capture warrant, and he started going between Germany, France, and Belgium until Angola acquired freedom in 1975.

do Ritmo, Cabinda Ritmos, Super Coba, Ngoma Jazz, Africa Show, Ases do Prenda, Aguias Reais, Bongos, do Lobito, and so on were the primary groups in Angola playing Angolan music before Angolan autonomy on November 11, 1975. These gatherings were situated in Luanda and Lobito in the Benguela area.

In the 20th century political instability and violence created an oppressive climate for Angolan musicians were oppressed by government forces,

Paul Mwanga

Paul Mwanga was a vocalist, and one of the early pioneers of soukous music. He was born in Angola. In 1944, when modern Congolese music was only in its earliest days, Paul Mwanga's music gained popular review among the local public. He began his career working in the company of seminal greats such as Wendo, and recorded a number of hits on the Opika Label teaming up with famous "Hawaiian" style guitarist Jhimmy (Zacharie Elenga).

Around 1950 or 1951 Nicolas Kasanda, later to be popularly known as Docteur Nico, made his debut singing behind Paul Mwanga.

In 1958 Mwanga signed to the young recording label Ngoma, which began a new period for him where his fame reached its height for his career. At the time he was one of the principal artists recording in the language Kikongo.

Eduardo Nascimento

Eduardo Nascimento born on 26 June 1943, in Luanda, Portuguese Angola was an Angolan singer, best known for his participation on behalf of Portugal in the 1967 Eurovision Song Contest.

Nascimento was the leader of a five-member band, Os Rocks, formed in Luanda in 1962. The band travelled to mainland Portugal in the mid-1960s, participating in song festivals and releasing a well-received EP, "Wish I May", in 1966. In 1967, Nascimento entered the Portuguese Eurovision selection contest, the Festival da Canção, as a solo artist with the song "O vento mudou" ("The Wind Changed").

He won the event by a comfortable margin, and went forward to represent Portugal in the 12th Eurovision Song Contest, held on 8 April in Vienna, where "O vento mudou" finished in joint 12th place of the 17 entries. With Os Rocks, Nascimento released another EP, "Don't Blame Me", in 1968, before giving up his musical career and returning to Angola in 1969.

Nascimento is notable for being the first black male performer at Eurovision, the year after Milly Scott from the Netherlands became the first black female to sing at the Eurovision. Nascimento passed on 22 November 2019.

Traditional Music of Angola

In the years just before the civil war, the Luanda rock music scene sizzled. One member of a top band said that being in a band then was like being in a top football team; when his band walked into a club, all his supporters would cheer and rival bands' groupies would hiss.

The acoustic guitarist Liceu Vieira Dias and his band Ngola Ritmos, is, however, the father of the most Angolan popular music, called semba. He introduced the ensembles of dikanza (scraper), ngomas (conga drums) and violas, which became popular in the 1950s in urban areas, where audiences liked the politicized messages and early nationalist thought. Dias was imprisoned by the Portuguese for many years.

Samba is the predecessor to a variety of music styles originating in Africa. Three of the most famous of these are Samba itself, kizomba, and kuduro.

▲ *Instruments of Angola*

The subject matter of Samba is often a cautionary tale or story regarding day-to-day life and social events and activities, usually sung in a witty rhetoric. Through Samba music, the artist is able to convey a broad spectrum of emotions. It is this characteristic that has made Samba the premiere style of music for a wide variety of Angolan social gatherings. Its versatility is evident in its inevitable presence at funerals and, on the other hand, many Angolan parties.

Samba is very much alive and popular in Angola today as it was long before that country's independence from the Portuguese colonial system on November 11, 1975. Various new Samba artists emerge each year in Angola, as they render homage to the veteran samba masters, many of whom are still performing. Other styles related to the Samba is Rebita, which is inspired by European line dances, as well as kazukuta and kabetula which are primarily Carnaval Music.

Barceló de Carvalho, the Angolan singer popularly known as Bonga, is arguably the most successful Angolan artist to popularize samba music internationally; it is generally being categorized as World music.

◀ *Manjeera*

Chapter 10

The Islands of Africa

East African Island – Zanzibar

Zanzibar is an island off the coast of Tanzania. The term Zang means "Land of the Blacks". The island is part of the Republic of Tanzania. It is composed of many small islands and two large ones: Unguja (the main island, referred to informally as Zanzibar) and Pemba Island. The capital

is Zanzibar City, located on the island of Unguja. It belongs to the World Heritage Site.

Zanzibar's main industries are spices, raffia, and tourism. In particular, the islands produce cloves, nutmeg, cinnamon, and black pepper. For this reason, the Zanzibar Archipelago, together with Tanzania's Mafia Island, are sometimes referred to locally as the "Spice Islands".

Historically, African populations from the main land populated the islands until the arrival of the Arabs, and Indian and Chinese mariners. The island shares a complicated history of successive takeovers from the Portuguese to the Arabs who created a Sultanate to the Germans and finally the establishment of a British protectorate. The total population living on the islands is approximately

1.3 million. In 1964 the Islands of Zanzibar rejoined the republic of Tanzania.

Musical Styles of Zanzibar; Taarab & Unyago Styles

Taarab is a musical genre that originated and became popular in Tanzania and Kenya. It is influenced and a fusion of the cultural and musical traditions of Tanzania, Uganda, Kenya, Egypt, and the Indian subcontinent. Taarab as a style was popularized in the late 1920s by vocalist Siti binti Saad. In Swahili culture, most notably in Zanzibar and in some areas of western Kenya, the word unyago denotes both a set of dance steps and music associated with traditional rituals celebrating the coming of age of young women and weddings ceremonies. Today we can still see Unyago rituals are practiced in East Africa but such dance steps have expanded outside of the religious to enter the realm of the secular.

Siti Binti Saad

Siti Binti Saad (1880–1950) was a pioneering artist vocalist in the Taraab genre of East African music. In an era in which male singers dominated, she was a pioneer as a woman singer in the genre. She was the first woman in East Africa to record her music in an album. In contrast to previous singers who sang in Arabic, she sang in Swahili. She sang in cities off the coast of Tanganyika (Tanzania) and Zanzibar. Her career peaked from 1928 to her death in 1950. During that time she recorded over 150 gramophone records in India. She opened the doors to more women entering show business and singing Taarab.

Fatima Binti Baraka

Fatima Binti Baraka aka Bi Kidude is a vocalist of Zanzibari origin. She was born in 1910. She has been called the "Queen of Taraab and Unyago music". She was inspired by vocalist Siti Binti Saad. Born in the village of Mfagimaringo, Bi Kidude was the daughter of a coconut seller in colonial Zanzibar. Bi Kidude's exact date of birth is unknown and much of her life story is uncorroborated, but she was believed to be the oldest touring singer in the world before her death. In 2005, Bi Kidude received the WOMEX award for her contribution to music and culture in Zanzibar. She was the subject of two documentaries by filmaker Andrew Jones. Fatima passed on April 17, 2013.

South African Island – Madagascar
The Island of Madagascar

Madagascar, officially the Republic of Madagascar previously known as the Malagasy Republic, is an island country in the Indian Ocean 250 miles off the coast of East and South Africa across the Mozambique Channel. At 228,900 sq mi Madagascar is the world's second-largest island country, after Indonesia. The nation consists of the island of Madagascar (4th largest island in the world and many peripheral islands. It is believed that Madagascar split from the Indian subcontinent around 88 million years ago, allowing native plants and animals to evolve in relative isolation. Consequently, Madagascar is a biodiversity hotspot. 90% of its wildlife is found nowhere else on Earth.

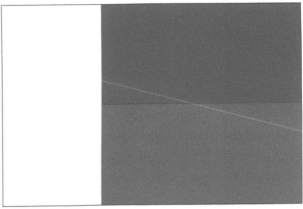

Its population is a combination mix of East African Bantus and Asian/Indian populations. For centuries the island was a vast cultural and maritime trade hub between the Swahili Coast of East

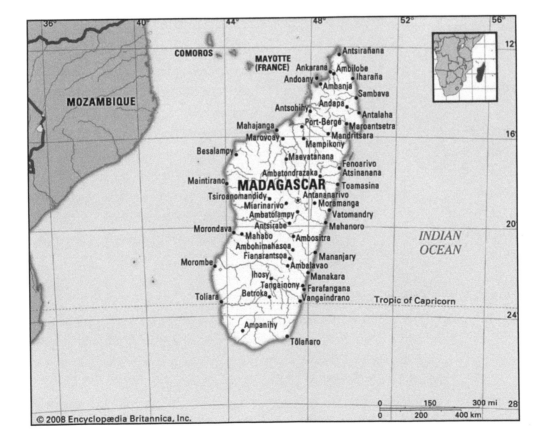

© 2008 Encyclopædia Britannica, Inc.

Africa, South Africa, the Arabic Peninsula, India and China for as long as it can be remembered. Its history is a succession of colonial attempts by Portuguese, Arabs and French conquerors. The island became independent from colonial France in 1960.

The capital is Antananarivo and its population count is 27.5 million.

Madagascar is the world's principal supplier of vanilla, cloves and ylang-ylang. Other key agricultural resources include coffee, lychees and shrimp. Mineral resources include various types of precious and semi-precious stones. Today, it provides half of the world's supply of sapphires, which were discovered near Ilakaka in the late 1990s.

Madagascar has one of the world's largest reserves of ilmenite (titanium ore), as well as important reserves of chromite, coal, iron, cobalt, copper and nickel. Several major projects are underway in the mining, oil and gas sectors that are anticipated to help boost the Malagasy economy.

Ethnic Groups

- Merina 26%
- Betsimisaraka 15%
- Betsileo 12%
- Tsimihety 7%
- Sakalava 6%
- Antaisaka 5%
- Antandroy 5%
- Others 24%

Religion

- Christianity 86%
- Islam 3%
- Traditional Religions 10%

It is a democratic republic with multi party representation.

Traditional Music

Vocal traditions in Madagascar are a blend of South African polyharmonic vocals and Polynesian melodic traditions. Musical performance in Madagascar has often been associated with spiritual functions. Music is a key component in achieving a trance state in tromba (or bilo) spiritual rituals practiced in several regions of the island, as it is believed that each spirit has a different preferred piece of music.

The association between music and ancestors is very strong on the eastern coast. It has led musicians to put valued objects inside a musical instrument (through the tone hole, for instance) as an offering to the spirits for the purpose of receiving their blessings. Music has been central to the famadihana ceremony (periodic reburial of ancestors' shroud-wrapped mortal remains).

Philibert Rabezoza aka Rakoto Frah

Philibert Rabezoza aka Rakoto Frah was born in 1923 in Ankadinandriana, a suburb of Antananarivo. His mother was born in Antananarivo and his father, a herdsman and farmer from Fianarantsoa had previously been a singer at the Merina royal court before French colonization in 1897.

Like many residents of the rural areas in central Madagascar at that time, Rakoto and his brothers played the sodina/flute, a tube traditionally made of bamboo. It is one of the oldest and most iconic musical instruments of Madagascar. His career began when he won first prize at a local music competition organized by the French authorities playing the sodina. Rakoto's opportunity for national fame arrived with the 1958 visit of French President Charles de Gaulle to Madagascar. This success was followed by performances in Japan, England, the United States, India, Germany, China, Norway, Finland, Australia and France making him one of the first musicians to perform traditional Malagasy music at music festivals and concerts outside of Madagascar. In 1985, producers Ben Mandelson and Roger Armstrong visited Madagascar in search of artists to record for a planned album of Malagasy music. Rakoto Frah soon came to

their attention, and they offered him a full-length album of his own. Malagasy guitarist Solo Razafindrakoto produced Rakoto Frah's Souffles de Vie in 1998, and Rakoto Frah's final album, Chants et danses en Imerina, was released in October 2000. Several collaborations between Rakoto Frah and other international artists have been recorded. Rakoto Frah is featured on tracks recorded with Manu Dibango, jazz artists David Lindley and Henry Keiser, Kassav', and Ladysmith Black Mambazo, whom he met while performing in India. He is remembered as one of the great masters of the instrument and torch holder of the Malagasy musical tradition. He passed in September of 2001.

Eric Manana

Erick Manana is an acoustic guitarist, singer and songwriter from Madagascar born in 1959. As a solo artist, singing in accompaniment to his acoustic guitar in the ba-gasy genre he gained prominence in the central highlands of Madagascar. In 1979, he left Madagascar to settle in France and settled in Bordeaux. His professional career as a musician began in 1982 as a member of Lolo sy ny Tariny. His first solo album was recorded in 1996. He was a member of the group Feo-Gasy alongside the celebrated master sodina player Rakoto Frah, and they toured Europe several times, promoting the traditional music of the central highlands of Madagascar. He has worked on a variety of collaborative projects, recording singles and performing with established artists such as Regis Gizavo and Solorazaf, and young breakthrough stars like Aina Quash. Most recently, Manana formed a group with another valiha player Justin Vali and other prominent Malagasy artists in the Malagasy All Stars. In January 2013, Manana performed at the historic Olympia venue in Paris to celebrate the 35th year of his career. At the close of the event, he was awarded the prestigious Commandeur de l'Ordre des Arts et des Lettres ("Commander of Liberal and Fine Arts") medal by the representative of the Republic of Madagascar to UNESCO. Rootsworld described Manana as the "Bob Dylan of Madagascar". He is the recipientof several awards, including the 1994 Prix Media Adami Découvertes at the annual Radio France International global musical competition and the Grand Prix du disque de l'académie Charles Cros in 1997 for his album Vakoka.

North West African Island – Cape Verde

Cape Verde Islands or Cabo Verde Islands officially the Republic of Cabo Verde, is an archipelago and island country in the north Western part of the Atlantic Ocean, consisting of ten volcanic islands with a combined land area of about 1,557 sq mi. These islands lie between 320 to 460 nautical miles west of Cap-Vert of Senegal situated at the westernmost point of continental Africa.

The Cape Verde islands were located in a convenient location to play a role in the Atlantic slave trade, Cape Verde became economically prosperous during the 16th and 17th centuries, attracting merchants, and pirates. It declined economically in the 19th century due to the suppression of the Atlantic slave trade, and many of its inhabitants emigrated during that period. However, Cape Verde gradually recovered economically by becoming an important commercial center and useful stopover point along major shipping routes. In 1951, Cape Verde was incorporated as an overseas department of Portugal, but its inhabitants continued to campaign for independence, which they achieved in 1975. Since the early 1990s, Cape Verde is a representative democracy. Lacking natural resources, its developing economy is mostly service-oriented, with a growing focus on tourism and foreign investment.

Its population of around 483,628 is mostly composed of mixed African and European heritage, and predominantly Roman Catholic, reflecting the legacy of Portuguese rule. A sizeable Cape Verdean diaspora community exists across the world, especially in the United States and Portugal, considerably outnumbering the inhabitants on

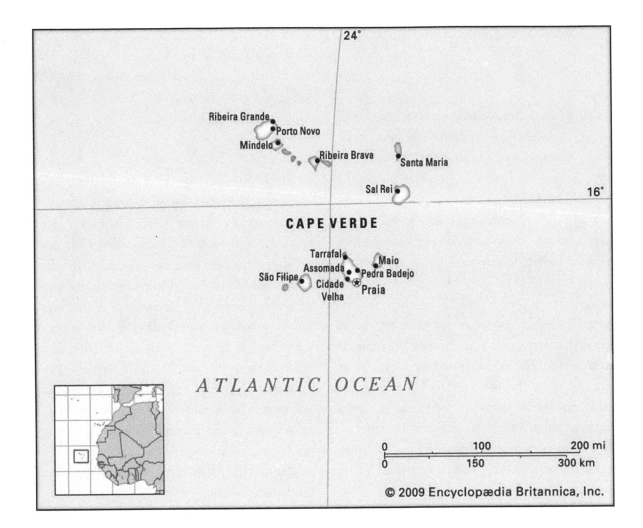

the islands. Cape Verde is a member state of the African Union. Cape Verdean's official language is Portuguese. It is the language of instruction and government. It is also used in newspapers, television, and radio.

Music of the Cape Verdean Islands
Morna

Morna is by far the most popular musical genre of Cape Verdean music. It has produced an international superstar in Cesária Évora. Morna is a national song-style beloved by Cape Verdeans across the many islands of the country. Lyrics are usually in Portuguese Creole, and reflect such themes as love and lust, patriotism and mourning.

The vocalists are accompanied by a cavaquinho (ukulele like), a guitar, violin, bass guitar and a piano. In the 1930s, Morna evolved in a swifter form of music called coladevincent. It is a more light-hearted and humorous genre, with sensual rhythms. Known performers include Codé di Dona, Manuel de Novas, Frank Cavaquim, Djosa Marques and Os Tubarões.

Aside from Évora, popular morna musicians include Ildo Lobo, Titina, Celina Pereira, Bana, Djosinha, B. Leza, Travadinha, Sãozinha, Maria

Alice, Carmen Souza, Gardénia Benros, and Assol Garcia.

Funaná

Funaná is an accordion-based genre from Santiago. Prior to the independence, funaná was denigrated by colonial authorities, who considered it African. Since independence, however, bands like Bulimundo adapted the music for pop audiences and Finaçon, who combined funaná and coladeira into a fusion called funacola. Other group includes Paris based LaMC Malcriado

Batuque

Batuque is also popular in Cape Verde. Originally a woman's folk music, batuque is an improvised music with strong satirical or critical lyrics. In the 80's, Orlando Pantera has created the "new batuco" (neo-batuku), but he died in 2001 before to achieve his creative work. Performers and songwriters are Orlando Pantera, Vadú, Tcheka, Mayra Andrade, Lura, Zeca di nha Reinalda.

Tabanka

Tabanka or Tabanca is a form of music in Cape Verde, also popular, it characterizes by having an allegro, a binary compass and traditionally being melodic only. Singers or artists and band include Os Tubarões, Zezé di Nha Reinalda, Finaçon, Orlando Pantera and Simentera.

Coladeira

Coladeira is a form of dance and music from Cape Verde. Singers and musicians includes Nancy Vieira, the band Simentera, Mité Costa, Bana, Manecas Matos, Cabral & Cabo Verde Show, Ildo Lobo, Djalunga, Paulino Vieira, Dudú Araújo, Beto Dias and Suzanna Lubrano

Colá

Colá is a form of music from Cape Verde. It is mainly sung during religious festivals in the islands of Santo Antão, São Vicente, São Nicolau, Boa Vista and Brava.

Cola-zouk

In the 1980s, the cape verdean diaspora living in Europe and North America have influenced the traditional "Coladeira" with Compas / Kompa to create a version of Zouk called Cola-zouk, a similar Compas (Kompa) fusion to the French Antillean's Zouk" or "Zouk Love". Later, the new generation who grew up in Cape Verde featured a slow mixed version of electric pop music with Cape Verdean music styles, a light Compas called "Cabo Love" or "Cabo Zouk". The Cape Verdean Zouks are typically sung in Cape Verdean creole, it is often mistaken for the Angolan kizomba. This light Compas has become popular in Portuguese speaking countries of Africa, Brazil, and the rest of the world. Most of the songs are written in Portuguese/creole.

Cape Verdean Zouk singers and producers include Suzanna Lubrano, Nilton Ramalho, Johnny Ramos, Nelson Freitas, Mika Mendes, Manu Lima, Cedric Cavaco, Elji, Loony Johnson, Klasszik, Mark G, Tó Semedo, Beto Dias, Heavy H, Marcia, Gilyto, Kido Semedo, Ricky Boy, Klaudio Ramos, M&N Pro, Gilson, Gil, G-Amado, Philip Monteiro, Z-BeatZ Pro, Gama, Juceila Cardoso and Denis Graça.

It is worth noting that from Jazz to Disco Cap Verdean musicians have contributed immensely to American music from NEA Jazz Master pianist, composer Horace Silver to Duke Ellington's sideman Jazz saxophonist master Paul Gonsalves to the hit machine disco band the Tavares.

Cesaria Evora

Cesária Évora, born on 27 August 1941 in Mindelo, São Vicente, Cape Verde came from a family of musicians. At the age of 16, she was persuaded by a friend to sing in a sailors' tavern. She grew up at the house in Mindelo which other singers used from the 1940s to the 1970s, at 35 Rua de Moeda. Other Cape Verdean singers came to the house, including Djô d'Eloy, Bana, Eddy Moreno, Luis Morais and Manuel de Novas (also known as Manuel d'Novas) and it was there she received her musical education.

During the 1960s, she began singing on Portuguese voyage ships halting at Mindelo and on the neighborhood radio. In 1985, at the greeting of Cape Verdean artist Bana, she went to act in Portugal. In Lisbon she was found by the maker José da Silva and welcome to record in Paris. She recorded the track "Ausência", composed by Yugoslav musician Goran Bregovic, which was released as the second track of the soundtrack of the film Underground (1995) by Emir Kusturica.

Évora's worldwide achievement came in 1988 with the arrival of her first business collection La Diva Aux Pieds Nus, recorded in France. Before that collection had been delivered, she recorded her first LP named "Cesária" in 1987. This collection was subsequently delivered on CD in 1995 as Audiophile Legends. Her 1992 collection Miss Perfumado sold north of 300,000 duplicates around the world. It included one of her most praised melodies, "Sodade".

In 1994, Bau joined her visiting band and after two years, he turned into her melodic chief up to September 1999. Her 1995 collection Cesária brought her worldwide achievement and the principal Grammy Award assignment. In 1997, she won the KORA All African Music Awards in three classifications, including "Best Artist of West Africa", "Best Album" and "Value of the Jury". In 2003, her collection Voz d'Amor was granted a Grammy in the World Music classification.

In 2006, Évora met with Alberto Zeppieri, an Italian songwriter, journalist and record producer and agreed to duet with Gianni Morandi, Gigi D'Alessio and Ron. The project, now in its fifth volume, gives visibility and raises funds for the UN World Food Programme, for which Évora was the ambassador from 2003.

Later in 2006, she released her next album Rogamar. It was a success and charted in six European countries including France, Poland and the Netherlands. On her tour in Australia in 2008, she suffered a stroke. In 2009, she released her final album Nha Sentimento which was recorded in Mindelo and Paris by José da Silva. The album reached number 6 in Poland and number 21 in France. In 2009, she became the first Cape Verdean to receive the French Legion of Honor by the French Minister of Culture and Communications, Christine Albanel.

She is the undisputed giant of Cape Verdean music. A vocalist of enormous command and charisma, she put the Cap Verdean islands on the world map. She received her last award at the 2010 Kora All African Music Awards, the "Merit of the Jury" award for the second time. Cesaria Evora passed December 17, 2011.

Manuel D'Novas

Manuel Jesus Lopes, poet, composer, songwriter was born in Penha da França in 1938, one of the neighborhoods of Ribeira Grande on the island of Santo Antão. He is the literary reference and one of the most important poets and composers of Cape Verde. His music is known all over the world, through performers like Cesária Évora, Bana and others. He lived in Mindelo on the island of São Vicente. He visited 35 Rua de Moeda where other Cape Verdean musicians visited including Bana. He took part in the 2003 Baia das Gatas Music Festival. Manuel passed on September 27, 2009. He is buried in Mindelo.

West African Islands – Sao Tome & Principe

São Tomé and Príncipe are authoritatively the Democratic Republic of São Tomé, and Príncipe is an island country in the Gulf of Guinea, off the western tropical shore of Central Africa. It comprises two archipelagos around the two fundamental islands of São Tomé and Príncipe, around 87 miles separated and around 155 and 140 miles off the northwestern bank of Gabon. The population as of 2018 is at 201,800.

© 2012 Encyclopædia Britannica, Inc.

There is a case that the islands were uninhabited until their disclosure by Portuguese adventurers in the fifteenth century; however that has not been confirmed. Bit by bit colonized and settled all through the sixteenth century, they aggregately filled in as an imperative business and exchange community for the Atlantic slave exchange. The rich volcanic soil and nearness to the equator made São Tomé and Príncipe ideal for sugar development, followed by cash harvests like espresso and cocoa. The worthwhile ranch economy was vigorously reliant upon enslaved Africans. Patterns of social distress and financial instability throughout the nineteenth and twentieth centuries of years finished in tranquil autonomy in 1975. São Tomé and Príncipe have since stayed one of Africa's generally steady and majority rule nations. The capital is Sao Tome, and the authority language is Portuguese.

Individuals of São Tomé and Príncipe are dominatingly African plummet yet there is a likewise critical blend of Africans and Portuguese relatives or mestiço. The prevailing religion is Roman Catholicism. Portuguese rule's tradition is also noticeable in the nation's way of life, customs, and music, which combine European and African impacts. São Tomé and Príncipe is an establishing part condition of the Community of Portuguese Language Countries.

The Music of Sao Tome & Principe

São Toméans are known for two very specific rhythms; Ussua and Socope, while Principe is home to the Dêxa beat. Tchiloli is a musical dance performance that tells a dramatic story. The danço-congo is similarly a combination of music, dance and theatre.

The hero of São Toméan popular music was the band Leoninos. It was created in 1959 by Quintero Aguiar. The group served as a spokesman for the people of São Tomé and Príncipe and promoted local culture. The band was banned by the Portuguese radio stations after it released "Ngandu" a song critical of the Portuguese colonialists.

Leoninos broke up in 1965, but were followed by Os Úntués, led by Leonel Aguiar, who added American, Argentinian, Congolese and Cuban musical influences, and introduced the electric guitar and other innovations. Popular music from the islands began to diversify, as bands like Quibanzas and Africa Negra. Among these groups was Mindelo, who fused São Toméan rhythms with Rebita, an Angolan style, to form Puxa.

In the latter part of the 20th century, songwriters like Zarco and Manjelegua found a domestic audience, and São Toméan-Portuguese musicians like Camilo Domingos, Juka, Filipe Santo, Açoreano, Gapa established a Lisbon-based scene.

Other 21st century singers who follow similar steps are Flavia, Bruna Lee, Marisyah, Calema.

Far Eastern Africa Islands – Seychelles

The islands of the Seychelles were recorded on March 15, 1503 by Thomé Lopes aboard the Rui Mendes de Brito, part of the 4th Portuguese India Armada commanded by Admiral Vasco da Gama. A transit point for trade between Africa and Asia, the islands suffered many colonizers from Europe, the Portuguese, the French and finally the British. In 1976, the Seychelles were granted independence from the United Kingdom and became a republic. It has been a member of Commonwealth ever since. Its Capital is Victoria and its population count is 100,000. The official languages are English and French. The Creole Seychellois is also spoken throughout the archipelago. The majority population is Roman Catholic (80%). Anglicans, Indhuists and Muslims share in the minority.

The Music of the Seychelles

Music and dance have always played prominent roles in Seychelles culture and local festivities. Rooted in African, Malagasy and European cultures, music characteristically features drums such as the tambour and tam-tam, and simple string instruments. The violin and guitar are

© 2012 Encyclopædia Britannica, Inc.

relatively recent foreign imports which play a prominent role in contemporary music.

The Sega dance, with hip-swaying and shuffling of the feet, is still popular; as is the traditional Moutya, a dance dating back to the days of slavery, when it was often used to express strong emotions and discontent.

The music of Seychelles is a reflection of the fusion of its multiculturalism throughout its history. The folk music of the islands incorporates African rhythms, African aesthetics and instrumentation, such as the zez and the bom (known in Brazil as berimbau) but also re-imagined European contre-danses such as polka and mazurka; French folk and pop; Sega from Mauritius and Réunion; Taarab, Soukous and other pan-African genres; as well as Polynesian, Indian and Arcadian music.

Popular African forms of percussion music such a Contombley, Moutya and a fusion of native folk rhythms with Kenyan Benga reign. Music is sung in the Seychellois Creole a mix of French and local language.

Conclusion

As I stated in my introduction the purpose of this book was not to try to chronicle the entire history of a continent for we know better but rather to begin giving an African lens to the immense variety of cultures and sounds that existed in Africa with a little bit of historical and political context. It is our hope that many authors will continue building and contribute to this academic effort as time moves on. This book belongs to Africa and African scholars.

We must begin by thanking the contributions of preceding scholars and their academic works coming from many different worlds of technical expertise, varied geographical spheres and intellectual dimensions for the more discerning directionality of their thinking and scholarship away from the vestiges of outdated western colonial mentalities. The preceding scholars such as Dr. Cheikh Anta Diop, Dr. Theophile Obenga, Professor Leopold Sedar Senghor, Professor Aime Cesaire, Dr. Louis Leakey, Dr. Mary Leakey, Dr. Franz Fanon, Professor Basil Davidson, Professor Marcel Griaule have provided us with the necessary academic architecture which has in turn allowed us to re-think Africa and its contributions to the world in a more chronologically sound and holistic manner away from the prejudices and the colonial mentality of the 18th, 19th and 20th centuries.

Africa the continent where humanity began, a continent and its people who in the last five hundred years have been subjected to the debasing pseudo academic writings of western nations, the atrocities and the holocaust of the Atlantic Slave Trade, followed by the colonial injuries of the Berlin Conference of 1884 and the insults of the post-colonial Cold War period continue to meet these seemingly insurmountable challenges one day at a time. Ordinary African men and women on the ground are facing the three foreign induced motivators of recurring economic afflictions through the never ending phenomenon of oppression, domination and exploitation.

These three afflictions have created an environment that continues to produce stresses of an unimaginable magnitude on its indigenous populations. Being the richest continent on the face of the planet has exacerbated these stresses as Western countries who have nothing in terms of mineral wealth in their respective geographical space have understood long ago that their long term survival is interconnected with their ability to continue mining African earth. As a result influential Western nations have devised and applied a significant number of financial and fiscal policies as well as military strategies for Africa designed to ensure their ultimate survival.

These socio economic and political stresses have largely been the results of the continuing Western world's effort in contributing to select African leaders which has in turn impacted Africans so much that their ability to modernize and rally around their own political wellbeing and economic priorities have been greatly diminished. Yet, despite the sociocultural, economic and political challenges Africans face on the ground their music from one side of the continent to another remains amazingly positive, uplifting and optimistic. It is important that Africans realize that Africa belongs to Africans as a whole, that the continent is not a warehouse for the Western world and that African governments are not subsidiaries of Western interests. It is this indomitable African faith in the future that will bring about the change the continent and the world desperately need, one day at a time, one battle at a time, and one more formidable generation after another at a time... and the best is yet to come...

Bibliography

Agawu, Kofi, Representing African Music, London: Routledge, 2003.

Allen, William Francis, Slave Songs of the United States, Dover, 1867/1995.

Berlin, Ira. Generations of Captivity: A History of African American Slaves. Harvard University Press, 2003.

Brown, Vincent. Reaper's Garden: Death & Power in the World of Atlantic Slavery. Harvard University Press, 2010.

Casely-Hayford, Gus. Lost Kingdoms of Africa, BBC Series 4, (2010)

Cesaire, Aime, L'Etudiant Noir, Journal #3, May-June, 1935.

Charry, Eric. Mande Music. University of Chicago Press, 2000.

Cheikh Anta Diop, (1959) The Cultural Unity of Negro Africa, Paris. Subsequent English edition (c. 1962), Paris: Présence Africaine, (1959). English edition (1978), The Cultural Unity of Black Africa: the domains of patriarchy and of matriarchy in classical antiquity, Chicago: Third World Press subsequent English edition (1989) London: Karnak House.

Cogdell Dje Dje, Jacqueline. Fiddling in West Africa. Indiana University Press, 2008.

Conway, Cecelia. African Banjo Echoes in Appalachia: A Study of Folk Traditions. Knoxville, TN: University of Tennessee Press, 1995.

Davidson, Basil. Africa Series, Davidson Collection, (1984)

Diop, Cheikh Anta. Precolonial Black Africa: a comparative study of the political and social systems of Europe and Black Africa, from antiquity to the formation of modern states. Translated by Harold J. Salemson. Westport, Conn.: L. Hill, (1987)

Diop, Cheikh Anta. The African Origin of Civilization: Myth or Reality (translation of sections of Antériorité des civilisations nègres and Nations nègres et culture). Translated from the French by Mercer Cook. New York: L. Hill, (1974)

Diop, Cheikh Anta. English edition (c. 1991), Civilization or Barbarism: an authentic anthropology Translated from the French by Yaa-Lengi Meema Ngemi, edited by Harold J. Salemson and Marjolijn de Jager. Brooklyn, NY: Lawrence Hill Books, c1991.

Donald C. Johanson (2009). Lucy's Legacy: The Quest for Human Origins. Harmony Books.

Dubois, Laurent. The Banjo: America's African Instrument. Harvard Publisher, 2016.

Finch, Charles III. The Black Roots of Egypt's Glory, Washington Post, Oct 11,1987

Freud, Sigmund, Moses & Monotheism, Knopf Publisher, 1939.

Gura, Philip F. and James F. Bollman. America's Instrument: the Banjo in the Nineteenth Century. Chapel Hill: University of North Carolina Press, 1999.

Haskell, Harry. The Early Music Revival: A History. Mineola, NY: Dover, 1996.

Hiebert, Paul. Transformative Worldviews, MI: Baker Publishing, 1987.

Horton, James Oliver. "Presenting Slavery: The Perils of Telling America's Racial Story," The Public Historian 21, no. 4 (Autumn): 19-38. (1999).

Ingman, M., Kaessmann, H., Pääba, S. & Gyllensten, U. Mitochondrial genome variation and the origin of modern humans. Journal Nature 408, 708 - 713 2000.

Jabbour, Alan. "Forward" In Transforming Tradition: Folk Music Revivals Examined, edited by Neil V. Rosenberg. Chicago: University of Illinois Press, (1993).

James Oliver Horton, Lois E. Horton. Slavery and the Making of America. Oxford University Press, 2005.

Johanson, Donald; Maitland Edey (1981). Lucy: The Beginnings of Humankind. New York: Simon and Schuster.

Leakey, L. S. B. (1934). Some aspects of the Kikuyu tribe. Man, 34, 59.

Leakey, L. S. B., Leakey, M (1965). Recent discoveries of fossil hominids in Tanganyika: At Olduvai and near Lake Natron. Current Anthropology, 6, 422-424.

Lidskog, Rolf. "The Role of Music in Ethnic Identity Formation in the Diaspora: A Research Review". Authors International Social Science Journal, Wiley Publisher. (2017).

Linn, Karen. That Half-Barbaric Twang: The Banjo in American Popular Culture. Chicago: University of Illinois Press, 1991.

Livingston, Tamara E. "Music Revivals: Towards a General Theory." Ethnomusicology 43, no. 1 (Winter): 66-85. (1999).

Lott, Eric. Love and Theft: Blackface Minstrelsy and the American Working Class. New York: Oxford University Press, 1995.

Mahar, William J. Behind the Burnt Cork Mask: Early Blackface Minstrelsy and Antebellum American Popular Culture. Urbana: University of Illinois Press, 1999.

Marquis, Colleen. 2008. "A History of History: The Origins of War Re-enacting in America." McNair Chronicles 1, no. 1: 1-15. (2008).

Mazow, Leo G. Picturing the Banjo. University Park: Pennsylvania State University Press, 2005.

Narváez, Peter. "The Paradoxical Aesthetics of the Blues Revival: In Transforming Tradition: Folk Music Revivals Examined", edited by Neil V. Rosenberg. Living Blues Journal. Chicago: University of Illinois Press, 1993.

Nathan, Hans. Dan Emmett and the Rise of Early Negro Minstrelsy. Norman: University of Oklahoma Press, 1962.

Obenga, Theophile. Ancient Egypt and Black Africa: A Student's Handbook for the Study of Ancient Egypt in Philosophy, Linguistics and Gender Relations, edited by Amon Saba Saakana, London: Karnak House, 1992.

Partner, Daniel, and Ed Simms. With a Banjo on My Knee: The Minstrel Song of Stephen Foster. Anaheim Hills, CA: Centerstream Publishing, 2008.

Perlman, Ken. Everything You Wanted to Know about Clawhammer Banjo. Pacific, Mo.: Mel Bay Publishers, 2004.

Ross, Pete. 1997. Civil War Era Banjo Instructor: Complete Lessons in Stroke Style Minstrel Banjo...Baltimore, Md.: Antebellum Banjo Music Publishing, 1997.

Sacks, Howard L., and Judith Rose Sacks. 1993. Way Up North in Dixie: A Black Family's

Claim to the Confederate Anthem. Chicago: University of Illinois Press, 1993.

Schwaller de Lubicz. R.A. The Temple of Man, Inner Traditions, 1998.

Senghor, Leopold, Liberte, Paris; Seuil Editions, 1964.

Southern, Eileen. The Music of Black Americans: A History. Norton Publishing, 1997.

Thiam, Pascal. From Timbuktu to the Mississippi Delta, San Diego: Cognella, 2013.

Thomson, Jeremy, Humans Did Come Out of Africa, Journal Nature, (2000).

Way, Amy & Herries, Andy, Australopithecus, Paranthropus, Australian Museum, 2020.

Winans, Robert. Banjo, Roots and Branches. University of Illinois Press, 2018.

<hr />

Chapter 3: Bibliography

Agbeyebiawo, Daniel (2000) The life and Woks of W.E.B. Dubois. Accra, Ghana.

Ames, David Watson. Continuity and Change in African Culture. Chicago: University Press. 1959.

Boahen A, Adu. 1990. General History of Africa. UNESCO.

Castles, S. and De Haas H., and Miller, M. 2014. The Age of Migration: International Population Movements in the Modern World. The Guilford Press. New York, London. Fifth Edition.

Chua, Amy (2002). World on Fire. Doubleday.

Chin, Weizu. 1975. The West and the Rest of Us. Vintage books.

Davidson, Basil. 1995. Africa in History. A Touchstone Book.

Diop, Cheikh Anta. 1987 Precolonial Black Africa. Lawrance Hill Books.

Diop, Cheikh Anta. Carlos Moore. 1987. Black Africa: The Economic and Cultural Basis for a Federated State. Chicago.

Diop, Cheikh Anta. 1981. Civilization or Barbarism. Lawrence Hill Books.

Freedom Time: Negritude, Decolonization, and the Future of the World. A panel discussion with Garry Wilder, E Balibar Etienne, and Gayatri Chakravorty, moderated by Bachir Diagne. Columbia Maison Francaise, Institute of African Studies, and Institute of Comparative Literature and Society. Columbia Maison Francaise.

Gellar, Sheldon. Senegal: An African Nation between Islam and the West. London, England: west View Press, 1982.

http://www.international-sufi-school.org/cab_thought_en.html

http://www.irinnews.org/report.asp?ReportID=53633&SelectRegion=West_Africa

International Monetary Fund, and the World Economic Outlook.

J. Ki-Zerbo. General History of Africa. Methodology and African Prehistory. UNESCO. 1990.

Kaba. Lansine. 1990. N'Krumah et le Rêve de l'Unité Africaine. Volume 11. Afrique Contemporaine. Chicago.

Kurian, Thomas. Encyclopedia of the Third World. Volume III. New York. Facts on File, Inc., 1982.

Macionis. John. 2016. Sociology. Pearson. Sixteen Edition.

Markovitz Irving. 1969. Leopold Sedar Senghor and the Politics of Negritude, New York, Atheneum.

Mazrui, Ali. The Africans: A triple Heritage. Little Brown. Boston.

Ndao, El Hadi Ibrahima. 2003. Sénégal, Histoire des Conquêtes Démocratiques. Les Nouvelles Edition Africaines.

Rodney, Walter. How Europe Underdeveloped Africa. Washington D.C.: Howard University Press, 1982.

Seck, Magueye. Lee Ann Hoff. 2009. Violence and Abuse Issues: Cross-Cultural Perspectives for Health and Social Services. Routledge.

Seck. Magueye. 2007 « Solidarité Pour Mettre Fin à la Violence Economique au Sénégal ». Notes from the International Colloquium on Migration. University Gaston Berger. Saint-Louis. Sénégal.

Seck, Magueye. 1987 Alcohol Use In Harmony And In Contradiction With Cultural Norms in Senegal. Boston: University of Massachusetts, Boston.

Tandian Aly. 2008. « Barca ou Barsaax « Allez a Barcelone ou Mourir : Le désenchantement des familles et des Candidats a la migration. Diasporas, Histoire et Societe, no9.

The Word Bank. International Development Association; International Finance Corporation Report. Africa Region. (FY2013-2017).

Washington. Booker T. 1995. Up From Slavery. World Classic.

World Bank. 2013. Country Partnership Strategy For The Republic of Senegal.

Zuckerman, Phil. 2004. The Social Theory of W.E.B. Dubois. Pine Forge Press.

Professor Pascal Bokar Thiam, Ed.D.

Faculty Appointment
Performing Arts & Social Justice
    Department, University of San
    Francisco, CA
Music Department, City College of
    San Francisco, CA,
Ed.D, University of San Francisco,
    M.Ed., Cambridge College,
    Cambridge, MA
Cert. Berklee College of Music,
    Boston, MA, Cert. National
    Conservatory of Nice, France

Dr. Pascal Bokar Thiam holds a doctorate degree in Education from the Graduate School of Education of the University of San Francisco, CA; a master's degree in Education/Music from Cambridge College, MA, a certification from the Berklee College of Music in Boston in Jazz Performance and certification in Classical & Jazz Studies from the National Conservatory of Region of Nice, France.

Dr. Pascal Bokar Thiam is a faculty in the Performing Arts & Social Justice Department of the University of San Francisco where he teaches courses in Jazz History, Jazz Improvisation, and African Music History. He is the director of the University of San Francisco (USF) Jazz Band. Dr. Pascal Bokar Thiam holds an additional appointment in the Music Department of San Francisco City College.

Dr. Pascal Bokar Thiam is a composer, guitarist, vocalist, faculty and author born in Paris, France who grew up in Segou, Mali and Dakar, Senegal (West Africa). He is the recipient of the Jim Hall Jazz Master Award for Guitarists from the Berklee College of Music, Boston, MA and he is the recipient of the Outstanding Jazz Soloist Award from NEA Jazz Masters Dizzy Gillespie and James Moody. He has performed with Dizzy Gillespie, Donald Byrd, Barney Wilen, Donald Bailey, Donald Brown, Art Matthews and more. His CD entitled "Guitar Balafonics" on SUGO Music Records received Downbeat Magazine "Best CD of the Year" Award in 2015 and a 4 Star review.

Dr. Pascal Bokar Thiam is the 2021 recipient of the Jazz Road Award from Southarts, the National Endowment for the Arts, (NEA), the Doris Duke Charitable Foundation and the Andrew W. Mellon Foundation. He is listed in the Great Jazz Guitars book by Scott Yanov published by Backbeat Books distributed by Hal Leonard Publishing. He is a headliner at major Jazz Festivals in the US and abroad and lectures worldwide on the topic of cultural transfers of standards of aesthetics from Africa that shaped the cultures of the Americas. Dr. Pascal Bokar Thiam is the leader of the Pascal Bokar AfroBlueGrazz Band.

Dr. Pascal Bokar Thiam is the author of the book entitled I Play in the School Band, Therefore

I am Smart, Bonn VDM Verlag/Publishing (2008) in which he studied and measured the quantitative influence of instrumental band performance on the cognitive development of high school students with a cohort of 120 students. You can find his work in the ERIC academic national library under School Band Experience on the Motivation of High School Students. He is also the author of the book entitled From Timbuktu to the Mississippi Delta; How West African Standards of Aesthetics Shaped the Music of the Delta Blues on Cognella Publishers (2011) with a foreword by NEA Jazz Master Composer, Pianist Randy Weston.

Professor Magueye Seck, Ph.D.

Professor Emeritus, Sociology & Criminal Justice
Ph.D., Brandeis University, M.A., B.A., University of Massachusetts, Boston

Dr. Magueye Seck holds a doctoral degree in social policy from Brandeis University; a master's degree in applied sociology, and a bachelor degree in economics from the University of Massachusetts-Boston. Dr. Seck served as the president of Emerge in Cambridge, a counseling agency for abusive men to curb violence against women. He also served for four years as Research Evaluation Specialist for the Massachusetts Department of Social Services. He co-authored a textbook titled: Violence and Abuse Issues: Cross- cultural perspectives for Health and social services (Routledge, 2009).

In 2006, Dr. Seck served as a Fulbright Professor at the University Gaston Berger of Saint-Louis, Senegal, his native island. He taught in French the theory and analysis of social policy, theory of violence, and theory of social justice. As a Fulbright professor, he organized the first international conference on "Emigration, Globalization, and Changes" at the University Gaston Berger in Senegal, initiating major public and academic discourse on poverty, inequality, social justice and immigration policies. For over two decades, he taught many courses at Curry College, including: Social Problems and Criminology, Sociology, Research Methods, Justice and Human Rights, Social Policy, Sociology of Violence, Social Statistics, Race and Ethnicity, Drugs, Sociology of Health, and Deviance and Social Control. Dr. Seck is the founder and moderator of the Annual Cheikh Anta Diop Round Table, at Curry College. In 2018, Dr. Seck became an Emeritus Professor at Curry College. He has taken on a challenging and supportive role as President of the "Saint-Louis Solidarity Association" in Senegal, leading the fight for social, political, and economic justice for the community of Saint-Louis.

CPSIA information can be obtained
at www.ICGtesting.com
Printed in the USA
BVHW010058040123
655467BV00018B/711